D0593967

Praise for *The Integrity Advantage*

"In *The Integrity Advantage*, Kelley Kosow's brand of brave insight and authentic wisdom gives you practical tools to reclaim your power, change your life, and be who you want to be. I highly recommend. Read it."

KUTE BLACKSON
author of the national bestselling book *You Are The One* and
world-renowned transformational teacher and speaker

"Kelley has the ability to elevate everyone that she meets into their highest expression. Her work transforms limitation in all forms and introduces people to the limitless power within them. I am honored to know her and to be able to call her my friend."

PANACHE DESAI
author of *Discovering Your Soul Signature*

"*The Integrity Advantage* is a powerful book that provides deep insights, invaluable skills, and step-by-step guidance to healing your fear, shame, guilt, anxiety, and pain of the past. Let this transformational book be your inspiration and catalyst to create the future of your dreams."

ARIELLE FORD
author of *Turn Your Mate into Your Soulmate*

"This powerful, personal exploration of integrity is a gift to anyone on a path of personal growth. I recommend it for its honesty and vivid examples of the power of living with integrity."

GAY HENDRICKS, PHD
author of *The Big Leap*; hendricks.com

"*The Integrity Advantage* cuts through any confusion you may have about 'what's missing' in your life. This special book will light you up from the inside out, igniting you to find your heart's desire. Pick this up today to discover exactly what you can do to truly improve your life from this moment on."

JENNIFER MCLEAN
creator of The Spontaneous Transformation
Technique and Healing with the Masters

"An empowering, freeing, heart-opening masterpiece. I loved it."

DR. JOE VITALE
author of *The Awakening Course*

"Like Kelley, *The Integrity Advantage* is funny, searingly honest, and filled with aha moments of wisdom that will surprise, inspire, and empower you."

MARY MORRISSEY
founder of Life Mastery Institute®

"Kelley Kosow has written an extraordinary book for anyone who wants to finally live life on their own terms. It will inspire you and it will empower you to transform integrity from just a word to a way of life."

JACK CANFIELD
America's #1 success coach and
coauthor of *The Success Principles*™

"*The Integrity Advantage* is a breakthrough book. Kelley Kosow makes an enticing invitation to what she describes as a whole new way of being in the world, illuminating the way to living a life of integrity."

GENEEN ROTH
author of *Women Food and God*

"With *The Integrity Advantage*, Kelley Kosow has hand-crafted a magnificent map to self-knowledge, truth-telling and wholeness—where all roads lead you right to you. As Kosow says, 'Once you commit to living a life from a place of integrity and self-referral, no other way of being will feel authentic or in alignment.' Using her own life experience and client stories as a through-line, Kosow guides you to find your own catalytic compass of courage and confidence within—to live in your deepest truth and attain your grandest desire. I not only urge you to read this book, but to live it with all your heart."

NANCY LEVIN
bestselling author of *Worthy*

"If you're ready to love, trust, and honor yourself at a higher level, *The Integrity Advantage* is for you. In it, Kelley Kosow offers up profound insights and deep wisdom from her heart, serving as a beautiful example of the gifts of living an integrity-guided life."

MARCI SHIMOFF
New York Times bestselling author of *Happy for No Reason*

"A master is not one with many students. A master is one who creates other masters. Debbie Ford's work and training on the human shadows was masterful. Her faithful student Kelley Kosow now continues Debbie's work in a loving way, and with great mastery. What an honor to Debbie. What a gift to the world."

IYANLA VANZANT
author and host of *Iyanla:
Fix My Life* (Oprah Winfrey Network)

the
Integrity
advantage

the
Integrity
advantage

STEP INTO YOUR **TRUTH**,
LOVE YOUR LIFE,
AND CLAIM YOUR **MAGNIFICENCE**

KELLEY KOSOW

sounds true
BOULDER, COLORADO

Sounds True
Boulder, CO 80306

© 2017 Kelley Kosow

Sounds True is a trademark of Sounds True, Inc.
All rights reserved. No part of this book may be used or reproduced in any manner
without written permission from the author(s) and publisher.

Names and identifying details have been changed to protect the privacy of individuals.

Published 2017

Book design by Beth Skelley

Printed in Canada

Library of Congress Cataloging-in-Publication Data
Names: Kosow, Kelley, author.
Title: The integrity advantage : step into your truth, love your life,
   and claim your magnificence / Kelley Kosow.
Description: Boulder, CO : Sounds True, 2017. | Includes bibliographical
   references. | Description based on print version record and CIP data
   provided by publisher; resource not viewed.
Identifiers: LCCN 2017004710 (print) | LCCN 2017020726 (ebook) |
   ISBN 9781622039470 (ebook) | ISBN 9781622039463 (hardcover)
Subjects: LCSH: Self-perception. | Self-esteem. | Self-realization. |
   Integrity. | Conduct of life.
Classification: LCC BF697.5.S43 (ebook) | LCC BF697.5.S43 K67 2017 (print) |
   DDC 158.1—dc23
LC record available at https://lccn.loc.gov/2017004710

10 9 8 7 6 5 4 3 2 1

To the amazing women in my life!

I am blessed to have you in my life—to learn from, laugh with, and lean on.

I particularly want to honor five very special women.

To my mother, Eleanor Kosow—your strength, style, and faith inspire me every day. I am in awe of the woman you continue to become!

To my three daughters, Chelsea, Nikki, and Ryann—I am so proud and lucky to be your mom. You are my motivation, joy, and love!

To Debbie Ford, a woman of courage, brilliance, and faith! You radically shifted so many people's lives—especially mine. Thank you for being my dear friend, my guiding mentor, and partner on the other side. Through your teachings, wisdom, honesty, and vision, you gave and keep giving me the gift of liberation!

Contents

PART THREE **The Integrity Plan**

INTRODUCTION Stepping Over Your Truth

Have you noticed something going on in our world today? I think I'd call it a trust crisis. People don't trust each other. We don't trust our neighbors, our bosses, or our politicians. We don't trust our families, our spouses, or our friends.

Why? Is it because everyone is corrupt? Just out for themselves?

No.

The reason we don't trust others is because, deep down, we don't trust ourselves.

That's right. Deep down, we don't trust ourselves.

Think about it for a moment. We don't trust our feelings, so we try to squash them. We remain in our comfort zone instead of going for our heart's desires. We don't trust the parts of ourselves that we think are unacceptable, so we cover them up. We ignore our inner voice and look outside ourselves for answers.

Our lack of trust, our tendency to look outside for what should come from within, leads to stepping over our truth. I'll use that phrase a lot in this book, and when I say it, I mean we don't trust ourselves. Because so often, when we make the wrong decisions, we do it knowingly. We see the truth right there in front of us. *He's not right for you. This job will suck the life out of you. You don't need to keep working; you've put in the time, now go home and be with your kids.* But we step over that truth. We don't trust the GPS inside us that will never guide us astray.

Think about the ways you have broken promises to yourself, leading to a pervasive state of distrust. You vowed to speak up at work, and then sat silent in the meeting yet again. You convinced yourself that this time you were going to stick to your diet, only to find the number on the scale inching up again. You committed to making a change, and then found yourself sliding back into the same behavior you'd been so desperate to avoid.

Even though we can sometimes undo something that has been done, or fix it in the outer world, the imprint it leaves on our psyche cannot be undone. It's like a nail and a piece of wood. If you hammer a nail into wood, you can pull the nail out, but the hole in the wood cannot be gotten rid of. It remains forever. We all have holes in our soul that represent the many ways we have betrayed, lied to, or disparaged ourselves—all the ways we have stepped over our truth. These holes serve as evidence to our already suspicious psyches—*you are not trustworthy!* And when we don't trust ourselves, we can't listen to ourselves. We can't heed the very guidance that our soul is trying to provide. We are cut off from the very essence of our being and end up living a life that feels wrong, inauthentic, and disconnected.

This book is an invitation to a whole new way of being in the world.

An invitation exists in every moment—actually, in every moment, a *multitude* of invitations exist, all dancing right in front of us, ready to be received, promising to shower us with new possibilities.

This book is an invitation to honesty, to being authentic with yourself, listening within, learning to trust and value yourself—your whole self, not parts of yourself. The good, the bad, and the ugly. I've learned firsthand the compromises we must make if we don't deal with the truth, if we ignore what we know deep down. We all know. We always know.

When we stop denying, when we stop being propelled by fear, we can finally start living a life of integrity.

Integrity isn't perfection. It isn't a strategy. It's a way of life. It's a way of being aligned with who we are and what we want. Being in integrity is the ultimate advantage. We can finally start living a life that feels right to us.

This book will help you get in touch with that knowledge and provide the support, tools, and inspiration to follow it.

✳

As Richard Bach wrote, "You teach best what you most need to learn."[1] My path toward integrity started with my being out of integrity when I was in my twenties. It was the day so many women dream of—my wedding day. The sun was bright, and the Miami heat was already settling over us as I sat outside by the pool in the lush, green backyard of my soon-to-be husband's house. As I sat chatting with one of my closest girlfriends who had flown in for the festivities, I was concerned about how the pictures would look, so I draped a towel over my face and even covered my eyes so I wouldn't get sunburned.

It was a day that was supposed to be full of promises. A day of new beginnings. My beautiful white dress was ready. The flowers were ordered, the cake was being adorned with handmade flowers, caterers were hard at work, and the makeup artist and hair stylist had cleared their schedules. Everything was ready for a meticulously planned, lavish celebration.

Sounds like my fairy tale was about to come true, right?

It wasn't. It was the day I made one of the biggest "mistakes" of my life.

It wasn't a "mistake" that I discovered in hindsight. Nope, I knew that day. I knew, on that morning, that I was making a "mistake." I qualify the word *mistake* because I truly don't believe in mistakes, since they are situations that are part of our divine plan and provide the foundation from which we grow and evolve. This "mistake" was the best thing that ever happened to me since it led me to this moment and provided me with the three things I love most—my daughters—but on the morning of my wedding, I knew I didn't truly love the man I was marrying, or at least love him in the way I should to commit my life to him. I knew he didn't treat me the way I wanted to be treated. There had been one red flag after another during our courtship.

But I was too scared to admit the truth.

Instead, I put that towel over my head.

Trying to distract myself from that voice inside of me, I kept my focus on the wedding pictures instead of the viability of the marriage.

I stepped over my truth and turned away from what I knew deep down. I decided to stay wrapped up in my plan and my planning instead of being honest with myself.

Have you ever done that? Gotten wrapped up in how things might appear instead of how they are? Covered up a gnawing feeling of doubt so that things could go according to plan? Put what others might think ahead of what you needed? Followed your head over your heart?

I had always been a bit of a perfectionist; my life followed a long list of things I knew I wanted to accomplish. Before my engagement, I had graduated from an Ivy League university (check!), attended law school (check!), and established a successful career as an attorney (check!). The next steps on my to-do list of life were marriage, children, and that white-picket-fence fantasy.

Within a few months of essentially declaring to the Universe that I was ready to get married, I met my future husband. And he was "ready" too. He was fifteen years older, had been married twice before, but didn't have children. He was ready to find the right woman and start a family.

We were set up through mutual friends. From the moment I met him, he reminded me of my father who had passed away when I was twenty-four, just three years before this new man walked into my life. He was smart, funny, and charismatic. He was a doer and go-getter. He was attentive, fun, and in charge, always arriving with a big idea or grand gesture. The first date became the second date and within days we were seeing each other every night. We met at the end of April, by mid-May he was talking about marriage, and by September he put a five-carat diamond ring on my finger. We set our wedding date for the following May.

A marriage proposal, a ring, and the ultimate little girl's dream, a wedding (check! double-check! and triple-check!). I felt like I had it all. That illusion did not last very long. Eventually, I'd wake up from the trance.

When we met, I was twenty-seven and he was forty-two. Although I had begun to build a career, he was much more established in our community, having worked and lived there for two decades. I was swallowed up in his world. Before I knew it, I was living in his house, socializing with his friends, and following the schedule and timetable he set for us. I stepped out of my life and into his. If he wanted to travel, we traveled. If he wanted to go out for a few drinks before dinner, I waited for him to get home. If he wanted to play tennis, we played tennis. If he wanted to have ten people over, I would stop what I was doing and entertain ten people.

As a person who likes alone time, I remember feeling like I was living at Disneyland; every minute there was a parade or event to plan for. If I said anything about this hectic atmosphere, I was either chastised for being antisocial or told that he was doing it for me so that I could get to know more of his friends' wives. After each confrontation, I backed off and went along with the plan. Sometimes I had fun, yet deep down I knew something was off.

Although I could focus on the wedding and stay silent about what was not working in our relationship, my mother could not. From the moment she met him, she disliked and distrusted the man I planned to marry. She struggled with our age difference and that he was, as she put it, a "two-time loser" when it came to marriage. I was to be wife number three. No matter how much she tried to talk me out of it, I wouldn't listen. She was so opposed to the wedding that she didn't attend my bridal shower, refused to help pay for the wedding, and even stopped speaking to me for a while. Having always been the dutiful daughter, defying my mother and remaining in the relationship with my fiancé was one of the most difficult decisions and emotionally draining battles of my life. On the morning of my wedding, I wasn't even sure she was going to show up.

My mother was right to be concerned. During our engagement, my fiancé and I had developed a toxic pattern. We broke up several times, but after each breakup, I was scared to death of being alone and veering off this plan I had for my life, and I ran back to him each time. I apologized profusely, no matter what the circumstances or who I believed was wrong or right. I said what I thought he wanted to hear, and wrote long-winded notes promising I would change and "it" would never happen again. I was reduced to begging, yet oddly enough, when he acquiesced to "give me another chance," I always felt like I had won!

A few months into our engagement, we started going to therapy. And although I am a huge proponent of therapy and learning tools that support people in communicating with their partner, we never got to the communication part. Our therapy sessions were like emergency surgeries to stop the bleeding caused by whatever blowup had erupted between us. It was like we were trying to make the marriage work for the sake of the children, but we weren't married yet and didn't have any children! There were so many times when I could have faced the truth and gotten out of what was already a toxic relationship, yet I kept plowing ahead.

If the beginning of a relationship is supposed to be the honeymoon phase, it was clear we were in trouble! We barely made it to the week of our wedding, but somehow I couldn't call it off even though my mother was hardly speaking to me. I was too scared to tell her or anyone else that I was dying inside, and I already knew I was making a terrible mistake.

So that May morning, I had a towel over my face in more ways than one. I hid under that towel when my fiancé would go MIA and could not be reached. I hid under that towel when people called the house but didn't leave messages. I hid under that towel when it came to finances. I hid under that towel when I ignored what I labeled as his "vices" and all of the empty promises that things would change—tomorrow. I hid under that towel when he stayed up all night emailing or talking to "business associates" on the phone. I had that towel over my eyes when it came to what I perceived as his unacceptable behaviors, excuses, justifications, and manipulations. I struggled to find "the truth" but completely lost focus as to what my own truth was.

The magnitude of my denial and self-doubt were huge!

I sacrificed what I believed deep down because I was desperate to convince myself that I had made the right decision or that someone or something would eventually fix it. (In all fairness to him, it doesn't matter what the actual "truth" was, whether my perceptions about him were accurate. Ultimately, it wasn't his behaviors that led me to being out of integrity—the fact that I stepped over my truth was the issue!)

Now almost twenty years later and having interacted with thousands of people throughout my career as a Master Integrative Life Coach, workshop leader, and teacher of personal growth and mastery,

I know I am not the only one who has allowed attachment to a checklist, the desire to be loved, or fear of change to be the impetus to step over my truth. Think of the times you have allowed yourself to accept the unacceptable. Think of the times you have settled. Think of the times you have silenced your voice. Think of the times you have given away your power. We have all participated in these behaviors throughout our lives, no matter how different our life experiences may be. I call it living in conflict with what we know deep down.

At some point, we finally say, "Enough!" when cheating on ourselves or selling ourselves out becomes too painful, when staying stuck and playing small is no longer enough for us, when we can no longer endure the old way of being because we know we are destined for so much more.

Here is the good news. If you are reading this book, you are ready—ready to step into the next, best version of yourself. How? Through declaring to yourself and the Universe that you deserve more, that you are ready to stop stepping over your truth and are ready to start living the life of your dreams.

I call this living a life of integrity.

A person of integrity is someone whose life isn't full of contradictions. They do as they say, and they say as they do. Who they are on the inside is who they are on the outside, and who they are on the outside is aligned with how they *feel* on the inside. They have declared what is important to them and who they want to be in this lifetime. The actions they take and choices they make are aligned with that declaration and reflect that they feel worthy and deserving to manifest that which they most desire.

Now, you may be thinking that integrity is a lofty, unattainable goal, where you must measure up to a certain standard of perfection. I'm here to say that is not the case. Integrity isn't a destination. It is a way of life. It is an internal guidance system that will never guide you astray!

We are all born with a knowing deep inside us—we realize when something is right or something is wrong. But we've learned to ignore that early detection mechanism. It's as if smoke alarms are going off in our house, but we've put in earplugs so we can't hear them. The house is burning down! Get out before it's too late!

Every time you bite your tongue, you swallow your integrity!

In this book, I'm going to teach you how to get back in touch with your internal GPS. I call it the Integrity Alignment Monitor, or I AM. When we learn to live in alignment with what we know deep down is right for us, we live in integrity. And living in integrity means we no longer live a conflicted, disjointed, insecure life.

Think about it. We work in jobs that we hate, stay in marriages that suck us dry, spend beyond our means, hide how we truly feel. We live in a state of constant conflict, always engaged in an internal tug-of-war. No wonder so many of us are walking around exhausted!

This book is an invitation to something different.

When I finally separated from my husband and divorced, people constantly commented on how great I looked. When they'd ask, "What did you do?" I'd reply, "I got divorced!" Later I realized that it wasn't the divorce that made me look and feel so much more vibrant and alive, but that remaining in the marriage and living outside of my integrity had fueled my self-sabotage and created my physical and emotional heaviness.

When we learn to stop stepping over our truth, we shed all the baggage that has been weighing us down. We can move forward into a life that feels right.

This book is a bit like a detox or diet. We are going to shed all the stuff that is weighing us down. Deanna Minich, PhD, author of *Whole Detox*, writes: "Toxins are better understood less as poisons than as *barriers*—obstacles to the life and health we truly want."[2] It could be a job that is not right for you, has never been right for you, but you are too afraid to change. It could be a commitment that you took on that you knew was wrong at the time, but you ignored that feeling because you didn't want to disappoint anyone. It could be a health issue that you want to avoid dealing with. It could be that relationship where you've been ignoring the warning signs for years.

The Integrity Advantage is about starting to live life on your own terms. It's about facing the fear, shame, and false beliefs that caused you to get into those situations in the first place and then starting to live your life according to *you* and from the inside out—because you are the only expert on you.

This book will help you face the big decisions like what job to accept or whether or when to have children. But you'll soon find that learning to live in integrity is a moment-by-moment choice. It can show you how to recognize the right choices for you in every single situation: what to order from the menu, what movie to go see, whether to say yes to that invitation or decide to stay home for some quiet time, or whether to be intimate with the person you have been dating. It will empower you to speak your truth in a neutral way, perhaps confronting someone who is gossiping about you or sending your meal back at a restaurant, without worrying that you will be judged for being a complainer or spoiled and entitled. It allows you to live a life without conflict, one that is whole and peaceful.

Whether it's our marriage, our health, our work, or our relationships, there is usually at least one area of our life where we willfully ignore or cover something up that doesn't feel right. That lack of comfort, that gnawing anxiety, that quiet but persistent voice in our head that's trying to warn us to change the course—those are all signals that we are living out of integrity.

And the problem is, the more we lose touch with our integrity, the more likely we are to continue to make choices that widen the divide, taking us further and further away from it. Think of it as being adrift at sea. Your integrity is the lighthouse on the horizon—when you swim toward the shore, the beacon grows stronger and brighter until, at last, you are home. But when you get too far from shore, the tide pulls you away. As you drift farther out to sea, the lighthouse grows dim in the distance. Eventually, you can't see its light at all, and you've lost any sense of the way back.

Once we let integrity guide us, everything becomes easier—clearer. It's as if we've been living in the dark, and then suddenly someone switches on a light.

That someone is you.

How to Use This Book

This book is divided into three parts. In part 1, I invite you into a unique understanding of my definition of integrity as well as what living in integrity is all about. We look at what I call Integrity Snatchers, those patterns that keep us from living in integrity. We walk through what it might look like to finally trust yourself, and then I introduce a powerful tool that you have within you to help you stop stepping over your truth. It's called the Integrity Alignment Monitor, or I AM, and we all have one. We were given one at birth, but many of us have never learned to use it. In this book, I'm going to show you how.

Your I AM will aid you in recalibrating your focus and point of reference from what is outside yourself to what is inside, so you can own and live from a place of inner guidance. In part 1, we also learn to tap into the benevolence of the Universe and come to understand how it is a powerful partner and guide, always by your side, giving you feedback, supporting you in seeing where you are out of integrity and what you need to handle in order to have your next evolutionary leap. Part 1 concludes with us each declaring, "Enough is enough!" as we digest what it costs to accept a life of mediocrity and then commit to the journey of *The Integrity Advantage*.

In part 2, we'll go through seven steps that will help you dig deep and uncover all of the negative thoughts, limiting beliefs, self-sabotaging behaviors, and nonserving strategies that have consciously or unconsciously compromised your integrity. It is like an internal cleansing, so you can finally begin living a whole, complete, undivided life. When you have gone through the process, you will have shed all the stuff that has been limiting you for years. You will come out feeling lighter, clearer, worthy of claiming your magnificence, and ready to dive into the third part of this book.

In part 3, we move from uncovering what is going on in your internal world to consciously crafting what you want to create in your external world. In this section, I take you through a five-step process that helps you clear out any clutter, chaos, or contradictions, so you can align with your deepest truths and grandest desires and manifest a life you love. Then, just as dieters need a maintenance program to sustain their new levels of fitness and well-being, I introduce you to the Integrity Protection Program, a set of structures and practices that will protect your highest vibration and support you in continuing to spiral up in worthiness, integrity, and acts and feelings of self-love.

Finally, we conclude with The Integrity Promise. When you choose to live your life in a state of integrity, you can finally stop compromising. You no longer deny parts of yourself that you have hidden away for years. You own all of who you are and feel complete, confident, and free to be fully yourself. You are finally able to change what isn't working in your life instead of plastering a smile over it. You are no longer settling for crumbs. You live a life that is 100 percent yours. And in that is great freedom.

To further support you in attaining this level of fierce confidence and authentic aliveness, throughout the book you'll find Integrity Insights and Integrity Igniters and my own as well as many of my clients' and students' personal stories.

Although our journeys are unique, our issues are often common to all. In the workshops and classes I lead, while I am the person on stage, I know that it is often the personal sharing of one participant that will be the catalyst for a breakthrough in another. All of the stories shared in this book are in service to your process. Be open to seeing yourself in someone else's story so that you can find a new level of compassion for yourself or gain a new insight about situations that may have occurred on your journey.

The Integrity Insights are powerful questions meant to support you in taking that U-turn back to yourself—to your I AM—so that you can start peeling back the layers of the proverbial onion, reveal what is going on, and start building your muscle of self-referral and self-trust. Let these questions be catalysts for thought, reflection, and journaling. The Integrity Igniters also aid you in tapping into your truth. Further, they involve actions that will assist you in integrating your insights and igniting your evolution. I suggest using a journal to give yourself plenty of space to dig deep into whatever is coming up for you with both the Integrity Insights and Integrity Igniters. You can copy the worksheets used in the Integrity Igniters into your journal, and they are also available at soundstrue.com/integrity-advantage/worksheets. Know that these worksheets can be used over and over again. As you evolve so will the situations you are dealing with as well as the wisdom you are ready to receive. The worksheets and questions used in the Integrity Insights and Integrity Igniters can be used as ongoing tools to support you in gaining clarity, finding your truth, or harnessing the power of the moment.

Remember, transformation happens in the heart and not the head. All of the parts, processes, plans, programs, and practices of this book are meant to take you from your head to your heart and to provide you with an experience of transformation!

part 1

THE INVITATION

1

A New Definition of Integrity

In most standard dictionaries, there are two definitions of integrity:

1 The quality of being honest and having strong moral principles

2 The state of being whole and undivided

For the first forty years of my life, I was only familiar with the first definition of integrity: the quality of being honest and having strong moral principles. Strong moral principles, I knew all about those; I was brought up by an Italian Catholic mother. She had a clear and strong sense of "right" and "wrong" and made sure to pass those concepts along to her three children. Being the youngest, and seeing my brother and sister punished for doing anything "wrong," I decided early on to take the path of "doing it right." My good-girl, overachiever persona was cemented before I hit first grade. I clung to my checklist of life, exceeding every goal and milestone I set. I showed up 100 percent and produced beyond expectation. When I became an attorney, that sealed the deal—I was a fighter for justice and truth. I, like so many others, wore *what I believed* to be my integrity like a badge, proof of my perfection.

From Shadow to Light

I did not become aware of the second definition of integrity until I met an incredible woman named Debbie Ford.

You may not be familiar with Debbie's work, but you will be after you read this book. She changed my life in so many ways, and I would not be what or who I am today if she hadn't come into my life.

Before her death from cancer at age fifty-seven in 2013, Debbie was a *New York Times* bestselling author, powerful speaker, radio host, workshop leader, and founder of The Ford Institute. A trailblazer in the world of personal growth, she was known for her expertise on something called "the human shadow"—what we deem unacceptable, have shame around, or just don't want to be. She was on the forefront of bringing the light of awareness to the parts of ourselves we keep hidden in the dark. In other words, she supported people in looking at themselves and their lives through new eyes, so they could break free from the prison of their past and stories of lack and limitation and create the life of their dreams. Debbie also created a life-changing program called The Shadow Process. It is a weekend-long workshop where participants learn to embrace all aspects of themselves. They discover how to own their smallest, weakest self as well as their strongest, brightest light and bask in the glow of unprecedented self-love and acceptance.

I did lots of transformational work before I met Debbie—I read books and recited affirmations, attended workshops, and posted mantras on my bathroom mirror. I attended rebirthing ceremonies, sweat in sweat lodges, had my aura cleansed by Indian shamans, and went to more psychics and astrologers than I care to list. I was looking for someone to fix me or give me answers! Although I encountered all kinds of wisdom, the shifts in my life still felt fleeting. I would make progress for a bit and then slip back into my old habits. When I first attended The Shadow Process Workshop, I saw my life in a radically different way. Instead of being the victim of my past experiences, I began to understand how they all came bearing gifts. There was wisdom in the wounds I had accumulated along the way, and I could either use everything that happened in my life, or it would use me.

Not only did my past experiences come bearing gifts, but so did the parts of myself that I had always seen as bad or imperfect. I had always felt the pressure to be perfect. I had spent my entire life striving to be smart, successful, talented, creative, and funny. In my mind, there was no way I could be weak, needy, selfish, vulnerable, or stupid. If I were, no one would love me. All those parts of myself, that were completely human and natural, were shut off. Instead, I kept perfecting and perpetuating my persona of the good girl, the strong, independent, has-it-all-under-control perfectionist and overachiever.

You may think, why would I want to be in touch with my weakness, neediness, selfishness, and stupidity? What is wrong with shutting those parts off?

The problem is, when we cut ourselves off from our whole being, we end up stunted, overcompensating for what we think we lack, and become extreme versions of certain characteristics. We risk becoming caricatures instead of complete, human, people. You can see this happening throughout society. Imagine the person who becomes a workaholic. They have no balance. They are run by their need to succeed and completely cut off from their ability to rest or be lazy. There is a time for everything in this life. There is a time for weakness; there is a time for laziness. There is a time for anger. In this book I'll show you how to access the entirety of yourself and understand the gifts each part can bring when you allow it to emerge at the right moment.

Because I was a perfectionist and overachiever, I was completely driven by my head and cut off from my heart. Things needed to make sense to me. It had to look good on paper or from the outside. That's why I could ignore all the signs about my husband. Our marriage made sense. It seemed like it *should* have worked. Never mind the way my heart felt in the presence of obvious disregard, incompatibility, and conflict. My head won out every time.

When I encountered The Shadow Process, I realized how much I sacrificed by living from my head and not my heart. It opened my eyes to how destructive it is to be completely detached from essential parts of ourselves and our feelings.

It planted the seed of what it might be like to live in integrity.

You see, the shadow represents the parts of ourselves we want to reject. Fearing that others will find out that at our core we possess "negative" qualities, we whittle away at those parts and create facades and personas to prove that we are not the things we dislike. This takes us out of integrity because it moves us further away from that second definition I mentioned: the state of being whole and undivided. Here are examples of how this can play out:

- The person who feels unworthy becomes a people pleaser. They do everything for others to prove to the world and themselves how worthy they are. They are completely shut off from their own needs, since underneath their facade they don't feel deserving enough to do anything for themselves.

- The person who feels unlovable or flawed because their parent abandoned them becomes the charmer, making sure that they are accepted and valued by all people. They are like bottomless pits when it comes to trying to fill themselves up with love and validation from others. Their belief that they are unlovable prevents them from giving themselves the love they need.

- The person whose parents came to America from another country and went from being well-to-do to poor becomes bent on not only fitting in but in showing the world how fabulous their life is with outward accoutrements like big houses and fancy sports cars. Their total sense of self is based on what is external since they never again want to feel the shame of lack.

- The child who is brought up more like a "trainee" than a kid has their list of activities, is overscheduled, and is pressured to excel in all things. Their need to be strong, independent, and special drives them. On the outside they look like they have it all together; on the inside they are suffering from anxiety and panic attacks.

When we feel incomplete and divided, we look outside ourselves for validation, but when we search outside ourselves for what we need, we end up living a life that is not *in*, but rather, is *out* of integrity. Until we face what we consider unfaceable, those parts of ourselves where we feel deficient are driving us.

Although the shadow is hidden, it is in charge!

The qualities we deem inappropriate or unacceptable aren't the only things we disown. We also disown our *light*—all of those magnificent qualities that we admire in others but do not believe could ever be inside us. Many of us are so used to the constant chorus of criticism and condemnation in our brains, a continuous, 24/7 soundtrack of negative thoughts, that it wouldn't dawn on us that we have everything within us that we truly seek. It doesn't seem possible.

For many of us, it is harder to own our brilliance, beauty, uniqueness, sexiness, and overall magnificence than it is to own our dark. We have been telling ourselves negative stuff for years, and we've been believing it. The positive stuff is harder to accept and own. It's like in the movie *Pretty Woman* when Richard Gere's character tells Julia Roberts' character that she could be more than a hooker, saying, "I think you are a very bright, very special woman." And she replies, "The bad stuff is easier to believe. Did you ever notice that?"

Enter Debbie

Before I went through The Shadow Process, I was cut off from many of my positive traits. Although I had accomplished a great deal in my life, I would never have said I was brilliant, successful, sexy, or creative. In fact, according to my upbringing, if I had *tried* to own those parts of myself, I would have been labeled a show-off and punished. Owning my light instead of seeing it as something to be ashamed of propelled me into a whole new level of confidence and consciousness. It was only then that I could access the power within me to leave my marriage.

Needless to say, The Shadow Process and the work of Debbie Ford catapulted me into a new calling in life. I immediately signed up to be trained and certified as an Integrative Life Coach. Eager to share the gift of liberation I had received, I immersed myself in my new vocation and became one of Debbie's most successful coaches. She invited me to join her staff. Before long, I was leading trainings and writing content for new programs. As Debbie's cancer took a toll on her body, and her energy began to wane, she gave me more and more responsibility. Soon we developed a close friendship. In fact, we spent a week together in

December 2012, shortly before she died. Although she had little energy at times, I thought it was a good sign that she was still buying expensive shoes. She planned to stick around long enough to wear them!

Soon after the New Year she was hospitalized. And then, even though she returned home, it became a possibility, even to Debbie, that she might never be able to get out of bed again. During her moments of strength, she started phoning the people she loved. I sensed she needed closure.

My turn came on February 9, 2013, at 9:40 p.m. I was in New York City visiting my daughter when "Debbie Home" flashed on my cell phone screen. Knowing that she was making these phone calls, and having missed my chance when she had called a few days earlier, I bolted out of a noisy restaurant to find a quiet place to have this important conversation.

As soon as I answered and heard Debbie's voice, I smiled. She sounded good, strong, like her vibrant self. How could she be dying?

She was eager to chitchat about my trip and my daughter. She asked about what we were doing and whether I liked my daughter's new boyfriend, declaring, "Next time, I want to come meet him." Part of me believed there *would* be a next time, but part of me knew she couldn't even sit up in bed. On the surface, it seemed a normal conversation, like so many others. Inside, I was aching for her to tell me something profound—some sage advice from a mentor to her student or some personal insight from one dear friend to another, but I knew not to selfishly spoil this normal moment. Debbie wanted to be my confidante instead of my dying friend, so I let her talk.

Finally, there was a pause. She had to catch her breath, and then she launched into the second part of the conversation: "Kelley, when I am gone, the vultures are going to come out. I want you to protect us from the vultures." I gulped. I didn't want to talk about when she was gone, but I had never heard her use the word *vulture* before, so I knew what she needed to say would help her to be at peace.

Debbie had written nine books and created an amazing body of work. She wanted it to live on, remain true and pure, and continue to impact the lives of thousands. She also wanted to make sure that I knew what her living wishes were—to safeguard the integrity of her legacy and make sure that those she loved and trusted would be able to carry on her work as she envisioned it. The fact that she saw me as part of that plan left me humbled, yet the reality that we were even discussing it left me nodding silently as tears rolled down my face.

Her breathing grew heavier and her voice fainter, yet she kept repeating, "It's all about integrity. You need to protect the integrity of the work. You need to stand in being the integrity holder."

"Of course, Debbie," I said, assuring her that I would do everything I could to protect her work and keep it alive in the world. I could tell she was tired and needed to go. We said our "I love yous," and she promised to call me in a few days.

I never spoke with Debbie again. She transitioned a week later.

As part of her final wishes, Debbie left the legacy of The Ford Institute equally to me and Julie Stroud, a fellow staff member and Debbie's executive assistant. I was deeply touched and incredibly scared to be given this much responsibility, but I knew Debbie had trusted me with it for a reason.

Many people described their last conversations with Debbie and the advice she had given them as a final gift. Sometimes she'd said, "Go ahead and marry him! Stop waiting!" Or other times she'd advised people on their careers. I hated to admit it, but at times I felt cheated. I wanted her to have guided *me* in our last phone call. Why didn't she tell me, "Marry that man"? Why didn't she tell me what we needed to do to run The Ford Institute and lead The Shadow Process? Why didn't she tell me, "*You are going to be okay!*"?

A few months later, I realized that she *had* told me what to do. She told me *exactly* what to do. I needed to step into the work she had always seen for me—the integrity holder!

A New Definition

It has been a few years since Debbie's passing, and turbulence and triumphs have ensued. There have been more growing pains and growth spurts than I thought possible. It has been a daunting undertaking and an amazing opportunity to try to sustain the legacy of someone so important, influential, and loved, while also determining the next path for her organization, respecting her grieving family and close friends, and trying to stay true to myself throughout this time! I have come face to face with more of my shadows and have had to delve that much deeper into the work I deliver for the fortitude and insight I need to stay clear and to connect with what comes next.

Swiss psychiatrist and psychotherapist Carl Jung is credited with saying, "I would rather be whole than good." The goal of doing shadow work is wholeness—owning all our characteristics, emotions, and experiences. Yet since that first workshop, after working with thousands of people and observing my own challenges and metamorphosis, I have come to realize that there is more to integrity than wholeness; you must take the next step of learning to live tuned in to the guidance of your whole being. Not only do you need to claim that you are full and complete, but also you must create your life from that vibration.

Being out of integrity means that something is off. What we are doing on the outside is not aligned with how we feel on the inside. Our life is not in line with who we are. It is filled with other people's wants and desires, things we think we "should" be doing, or stuff that doesn't mean anything to us. A life that is out of integrity means a life that feels incongruous, out of alignment, inauthentic—off.

We make decisions based in lack instead of wholeness, fear instead of truth, and in the confines of our comfort zone instead of the vastness of our grandest vision.

When I understood that, I saw the connection between wholeness, truth, and vision and the new definition of integrity:

- If we cannot own that we are whole and complete, we are out of integrity.

- If we are stepping over our truth, we are out of integrity.

- If we are not living in the vision of our heart's desires, we are out of integrity.

My new definition of integrity became this:

> Integrity is owning all of who we are and living in
> alignment with our deepest truths and grandest desires.

That's right. Step one was what Debbie was tackling with shadow work. And we'll cover a lot of that here. But there is another level to living in integrity—it is learning to live in alignment with our deepest truths and grandest desires.

It's time to get back in touch with your inner GPS. To live an integrity-guided life means that you stop looking outside yourself for validation, for guidance, for meaning, and for love.

*

Integrity isn't something you decide to do. It isn't someplace you get to. It isn't a badge or title you wear. Defining and living in your integrity isn't about achieving a goal or doing anything and expecting some reward—although you will achieve more than you ever thought possible and feel completely content. Ultimately, integrity is not defined by a state of *doing*. Integrity is a state of *being*. Integrity is not a result or destination, but a way of life.

There's a saying I love based on the writings of Ralph Waldo Emerson: Who you are speaks so loudly I can't hear what you're saying. Who you are *being* is your integrity. It isn't our actions, words, and achievements that define our life or our integrity; our state of being defines our integrity, and our actions, words, and achievements are a manifestation of that state of being. Owning that our beingness is whole and complete, and stepping into that, we feel deserving enough to live in our deepest truths and in the light of our grandest desires. This fuels us in a way that we never thought possible. You'll find yourself on the top of your to-do list when it comes to taking actions and making choices, not wondering what others need, but what feels right to you.

Everything that we need is inside us. I'm going to show you how to find it. We've got to understand a few things first.

2 Integrity Snatchers

So exactly how have we gotten so out of touch with all the beauty and goodness inside us? How have we lost trust in who we are deep down? Why aren't we constantly checking in with ourselves and living a life of integrity?

Humans are meaning-making machines. Anytime something happens in our life, whether we had control over it or not, we attach a meaning to it. If you stuttered when you got up to read in front of your third-grade class, and the other kids laughed at you, you might have interpreted it as *I am stupid* or *It's not safe to be seen.* If a parent abandoned you when you were young, you might have made it mean *I am unlovable.* If you were the last one picked for a sports team or not invited to a party, you probably thought *Something is wrong with me* or *I am not good enough.* If you were sexually abused or even had a serious illness, you might have decided that you are *damaged* or *broken.* We even do it as adults. If you get divorced in your forties, you might automatically presume *I'm not attractive anymore. I'll be alone for the rest of my life. I have messed up my children forever.*

But go back and read all those thoughts. None of them are the "truth," are they? They are interpretations that your meaning-making machine created. And look again. There is one thing all these "meanings" hold in common. They are negative. They often begin with "I'm not . . ." and are infused with doom and gloom and adverse perceptions of yourself and the world. The meaning-making machine automatically attaches a negative connotation to whatever happens, even if a divorce (like mine) can be the best thing to ever happen to you!

Because your meaning-making machine colors your perception of your life and your very self, and can dictate your actions, nonactions, and choices, you probably live with some constant companions. I call them Integrity Snatchers. Integrity Snatchers diminish your sense of self and erode your self-trust. They are not "bad" or "wrong." They are not something to be gotten rid of since they are part of our humanity, and if you are human you won't be able to get rid of them. But the important thing is to become aware of them and to understand that when left unattended, Integrity Snatchers will keep you from making the highest choices for yourself and going for the life of your dreams.

When you become aware of your Integrity Snatchers, you can remove them from their seat of power.

INTEGRITY SNATCHER 1   Shame

As humans, we are desperately afraid that the negative labels we have given ourselves are true. And thus, shame arises. We are paralyzed by the shame of believing that we are not good enough, strong enough, smart enough, or pretty enough. Our shame, which is generally birthed from some childhood event, teaches us to hide who we truly are because we fear that who we are is fundamentally flawed. Our shame leads us to believe that people won't like us if they know who we truly are at our core. Our shame is what creates our external persona and robs us of authenticity.

Have you heard Brené Brown's saying? "Guilt says, I *made* a mistake. Shame says, I *am* a mistake."[1] Shame can be the most painful emotion of all. When we are ashamed, we don't see the qualities buried in that shame as being *part* of who we are; instead we see them as *all* of who we are. We overidentify with the parts of ourselves we like the least. With this narrow view of self, we walk around thinking things like *I am the dumb one in the group. I am the fat friend. I am the one who is unlucky in love.* In The Shadow Process, we do an exercise using what we call "shame chips," signs that have sayings on them like, "I'm not good enough," "I don't belong," "I'm unworthy." When I ask a room full of people if they think they deserve a particular sign or shame chip, dozens of hands shoot up. People actually fight for the right to tell you how unlovable, undeserving, or broken they truly are. This is all a result of their shame.

Shame keeps us from seeing that we are whole and complete. *Believing that we are our shame, fundamentally flawed, need fixing, are not to be trusted, and must hide, we dull down our desires and don't strive for amazing.* Why? Because we don't believe we deserve amazing or can achieve amazing. Above all, we don't want to feel the pain of our shame if we risk something and fail. The time bomb of our shame is ticking loudly and keeps us stuck and playing small. It leaves us paralyzed, fearing rejection, expecting disappointment, hiding who we are. It keeps us from reaching for the life we dream of and know we are meant to live. Our shame is at the core of all our other Integrity Snatchers, especially Integrity Snatcher 2, the shadow.

INTEGRITY SNATCHER 2 Shadow

Our shame gives birth to our shadow. As I discussed in chapter 1, our shadow is comprised of the parts of ourselves that we have so much shame around that we disown. We judge ourselves so relentlessly that we cannot fathom the possibility that our shadow aspects or unwanted characteristics live inside us. *How could I be weak, a door-mat like my mother? A cheater or liar like my ex? Or mean and abusive like my father?* Because our negative qualities and characteristics are so distasteful or symbolize someone who hurt us deeply, we disown and detach from them. We vow to ourselves that we are not and never will be that! Our need to bury these parts of ourselves, and deny their existence, automatically wreaks havoc on our integrity. We cannot be whole and complete if we have lost access to the full spectrum of our traits and emotions. We cannot live in our truth if we are hiding the existence of all these parts of ourselves from ourselves and others.

INTEGRITY SNATCHER 3 Fear

Our shame, our belief that *I am that . . .* gives birth to our shadow, our insistence that *I don't want to be that . . .*, which gives birth to another

Integrity Snatcher—living in a constant state of fear. We are afraid at every moment of our life that someone might discover our faults and unworthiness! This, coupled with that negative meaning loop that keeps playing in our minds, paralyzes us. We view life through a lens of fear. Our fear permeates every area of our being. We have fears about ourselves: *I'm not good enough, pretty enough, competent enough.* We have fears about life: *Life is unfair. Life is about struggle.* We have fears about others: *People will disappoint me. I can't trust anyone. Everyone leaves.* We have fears even about the "good stuff": *Love hurts. There is no such thing as happiness. Nothing lasts forever.*

This constant state of fear becomes our baseline state of being—the place from which we interpret life, generate thoughts and feelings, and determine actions and behaviors. A huge percentage of my clients work with me because they are frozen by their fear and have been for years and sometimes even decades. They have stayed in marriages because of financial fear, fear of being alone, or fear of judgment. They have not pursued their dreams or taken chances out of fear of failing or fear of change. They have remained in the background out of fear of being embarrassed or fear of being seen. Others are stuck because no matter which way they turn, their fear smacks them in the face. They have fear of being invisible as well as fear of being visible. They fear sounding dumb as well as sounding too smart. They fear being successful as well as being unsuccessful. They fear being in love and loving because they fear falling out of love and feeling unlovable. They fear moving in either direction, and so they don't move in any direction!

By living in our cloud of fear, we often experience the loss or rejection that we most fear because our fear doesn't only paralyze us but it also separates us. We separate ourselves from others fearing that they will find out that we are not lovable or deserving. We separate from our day-to-day reality by checking out and engaging in all of our addictive behaviors that keep us from feeling our pain, shame, and fear. We separate from our integrity—from our deepest truths—because we are so afraid to let them be known or that others will judge us. We separate from our grandest desires because we are so fearful that they will never happen or that we don't have what it takes to manifest them. Unfortunately, this unconscious strategy of trying to separate from what we fear only results in diminished levels of self-trust, and more pain, and—fear!

We cannot protect ourselves forever from illness, accidents, the loss of love, or our own death. If we think about it, we have already lived through many of our greatest fears. We are survivors! Yet, fear is probably the most insidious of the Integrity Snatchers because it permeates every thought and becomes part of the narrative for the next Integrity Snatcher: your story.

INTEGRITY SNATCHER 4   Your Story

Each of us has a story. We actually have many stories. They consist of all the thoughts, beliefs, internal dialogues, and fears that we have around any subject. For example, our story lines can range from anything like *I will never get what I want* to what your fate will be based on your gender, color of your skin, level of education, or even your weight. Our stories stem from all the meaning-making that we set into motion as a child. We can also adopt the stories of the communities we grow up in or the people closest to us. Many of us take on the stories of our parents. They can become the narrative of the family that gets passed down from generation to generation, anchoring the family in a legacy of lack. Although these stories are not necessarily bad or good, they can be limiting.

We can also step into the stories of who others believe us to be. Like an actor being cast in a scene, we take on the role of the character we are made to play or feel compelled to play to ensure our part in the movie. When we overidentify with these caricatures, we lose sight of who we truly are.

Our stories—the ones we develop as well as the ones we inherit or are cast in—detail the person we know ourselves to be. We live the plotline assigned to our character. *I am the family screw-up, so I always mess up. I am the rebel, so I never can conform and cannot do anything without a fight. I am the good girl, so I do everything for everybody, and I do it perfectly.* Our stories tend to dictate our life. This is especially true when it comes to the stories of how we define ourselves, who we believe ourselves to be, or what we think we can or cannot have or achieve. Our stories are predicated on the past, impact the present, and become self-fulfilling prophecies for the future. Like the movie *Groundhog Day*, our stories tend to repeat themselves over and over again and often have the same endings.

Susan was a client who almost ruined her second marriage because she could not step out of her "I don't belong" story. Having grown up in a family that moved around a lot, Susan never had many friends. Just as she would get to know a handful of children in her school or neighborhood, it would be time for her parents to move again. Because of all the upheaval, her story was centered around her belief that she did not belong. Even though she was outgoing and seemed to attract friends, Susan never felt a real connection to people or that they were there for her. Aching to fit in somewhere, Susan got married when she was young. The fact that she was too immature to be married, coupled with her belief that no one was there for her, doomed the marriage from the start, and it ended quickly.

Not long after her divorce, Susan met Mark. He was a kind man who had two children from a previous marriage who lived with him most of the time. Susan loved living with Mark and his kids. For the first time in her life, she felt needed, wanted, and like she belonged. Susan and Mark had a daughter together, and that was the icing on the cake. Susan busied herself in her role of wife and mother and nested in her sense of belonging. Everything was perfect until Mark's ex-wife came back into the picture and wanted to play a more significant role in her children's lives. The children, who were now teens, were thirsty for a relationship with their mother and jumped at the chance. Mark, who felt bad about his children having been abandoned by their mother, bent over backward to accommodate his ex-wife's requests and the children's desires.

When Susan contacted me, she was livid! She felt betrayed and let down and like Mark and his children were suddenly playing for the other team. On Susan's scorecard, it was Susan and their daughter on one side, and Mark and his two children on the other. Underneath Susan's anger was deep sadness. She could no longer stand the pain of feeling rejected and disappointed by everyone she cared for and loved. Once again she felt like she didn't belong.

Shortly after we started working together, I tried to show Susan what her story was doing to her beautiful life. No one had ever told her she didn't belong; instead, Susan had given herself this designation. She was the one who created and was perpetuating her "I don't belong" story, and that story was actually pushing others away, creating her feelings of separation and causing so much of her pain. Susan began to realize how she was passing this story on to her daughter, pitting her against her half-brother and sister, and instilling in her sweet child the very feelings that Susan had battled her entire life.

Susan was finally able to see what was happening in the light of truth: her step-children just wanted a relationship with their biological mother. She realized that all the love that she wanted was still there for her, and if she wanted this chapter to end differently, all she needed to do was to step out of her story of the past and into the reality of her present.

Our stories can rob us of the happiness that is right there waiting for us. We all have them. We probably can't fully get rid of them, but we can see them for what they are. We can choose to step out of them and begin to live in integrity instead of in reaction to a myth.

INTEGRITY SNATCHER 5
Playing the Role of the Victim

Like Susan, when we are stuck in our stories, we are generally cast in the role of the victim. But when we vow to live a life of integrity, we commit to live a life of radical responsibility. We acknowledge that our life is in our hands. It is a demarcation point—a gift we give to ourselves. It means we take our power back. It means being responsible for our thoughts, beliefs, choices, and behaviors and for our deepest dreams and grandest desires. There is no sustained room for, *Oh, woe is me! Poor me! Forget about me!* or *You did this to me!*

Our tendency to want to blame others and play the role of the victim derails our dreams, diminishes our source of power, and erodes our integrity. When we stand in this place of powerlessness:

- We are not owning all of who we are, but focusing on a small part of who we are or are not.

- We are not claiming our role as a co-creator of our life, but living deep inside a story of victimization.

- We are not living our truth, but drowning in the resignation of not having the power to change things.

- We are not standing steadfast in our desires, but sinking in the black hole of our excuses.

- We are not connected to and trusting in the Divine design of the Universe, but feeling divided and defensive as if everything is being done to us, instead of *for* us.

To get back into integrity, we need to stop pointing one finger at everyone else and look at the three fingers pointed back at ourselves. We need to stop blaming and looking at what others are doing or not doing and take responsibility for what *we* can do. As George Bernard Shaw wrote, "I hear you say 'Why?' Always 'Why?' You see things; and you say 'Why?' But I dream things that never were; and I say 'Why not?'"[2] To go from victim to co-creator, we must go from *Why?* to *Why not?* We need to stop waiting for someone else to fix things and instead tell the truth about how we participated in the situations in our life. It is only then that we can find the lessons, declare what is important to us, and look within to determine what is next.

Here's another example: Eric had become the victim of his own success. A whiz with numbers and having a photographic memory, he was always at the head of his class. No one was surprised when he attended a top-notch university, worked on Wall Street, and went on to graduate school to get an MBA. During this time, Eric married and had a daughter and a son.

Eric rose in the ranks of the brokerage firm where he worked. Eventually, he started his own company, reaching ever higher levels of success. But because he was determined to continue to add to his accomplishments, Eric worked around the clock. He traveled frequently and missed many of his son's soccer games and his daughter's ballet recitals. Time flew by, and his children were in high school. Before long they would be leaving for college, and Eric had been absent for most of their lives. When a larger firm offered to buy Eric's company, he decided it was time. But one of the stipulations of the sale was that Eric stay on and run his company until a suitable replacement was found. The company promised that the longer Eric stayed, the more of his stock options vested.

Six months passed and then a year. The new company was thriving with Eric's participation. Yet with each day that passed, his children were one day closer to going away to college. Finally, his wife asked, "Didn't you sell your company so you could spend more time at home?" Eric claimed that the company needed him—plus they were making so much money, so he stayed on.

Eventually, Eric realized that he had become the "poor little rich boy." He had the right to retire or carve out a new deal at any time. He was claiming to be the victim when he had it in his power all along to do what was best for his family. Finally, Eric took control of his fate and moved to an advisory capacity in the company. This allowed him to spend more time enjoying life with his family. He felt full and without regret when the day came to take his children to college. By assuming responsibility for his actions, Eric became the father he aspired to be.

Not only did casting himself in the role of the victim compromise Eric's integrity, but being in the space of wanting—wanting more prestige, power, and money—violated his integrity. Wanting is another Integrity Snatcher.

INTEGRITY SNATCHER 6 Wanting

Wanting is the Integrity Snatcher I'm most vigilant about because anytime I am in a place of wanting, I can slip and slide right out of my integrity. Especially when I think about the men in my life—wanting for him to be the one, wanting to make the relationship work, wanting to hold on and not let go, not wanting to hurt someone's feelings—I can't tell you how many times I stepped over my truth and out of my integrity in order to fuel the fantasy and turn the *wanting* into my reality.

Wanting comes from fear or lack. Whether we are conscious of it or not, we think we are missing something, so we yearn for the outside world to fill us up. It is our fear and our wounded and diminished sense of self telling us that we don't have something and that we need to get it. That need turns to desperation, and the cliché is true—desperate people do desperate things. They ignore their truth as well as all the warning signs. They buy into their own BS and put themselves into scenarios that they often know won't end well, but they can't help themselves—they *wanted* it so badly.

Maybe you want your fairy-tale ending like me, and so you ignore the warning signals of a toxic relationship. Maybe you want the "perfect" body, so you starve, overexercise, purge, or engage in unhealthy habits to achieve what you think will make you look better. Maybe you want what you believe is "best" for someone you love, and your attachment to your agenda overshadows listening to and honoring their needs and desires, ultimately pushing away the one you wanted to keep closest.

There is nothing wrong with wanting something. But when we become so fixated on getting what we want that we sacrifice everything else, that is when we get out of integrity.

Wanting love, wanting material possessions, wanting accolades or attention from others, or wanting validation from the outside world all come from a sense of deficiency and despair. If we recognized our fullness, embraced our wholeness, and were connected to ourselves and the Universe, we would be able to stand in faith and trust time.

After a very painful (but powerful) breakup, I developed sciatica. The discomfort was so excruciating that I could hardly move my right leg. I literally had to lift it with two hands to step over my computer cord. Lying on the physical therapist's table, I realized that every time I wanted, like in this relationship, I ignored the warning signs and kept moving forward. I realized the Universe was trying to teach me a lesson.

By not allowing me to physically lift my leg, I could no longer step over my truth to reach my wanting. After six months of chronic pain, once I received that message, the discomfort in my leg began to subside.

Wanting others to fill our cup is a surefire path to disempowerment and disappointment. We can never feel truly safe and secure if the source of our happiness is based on something outside ourselves. When we do this, we give away our power. We become dependent on others. We become a feeder—someone who is wanting and trying desperately to get their needs met by others. Anytime you are looking to another person for validation, approval, to love you, you are feeding off them. We feed off others because we are not giving ourselves the nourishment we need. We must learn to fill our own cup.

And the thing about being a feeder is that for every feeder, for every person who is looking to give their power away, there is someone willing to empower your helplessness.

INTEGRITY SNATCHER 7
People Who Empower Your Helplessness

Although integrity is an inside job, and not something others can give to or take away from us, we all are human. At some point, we might want someone to take care of us, to assist us, to save us, or to handle a part of our life that we don't feel confident in or enjoy. So this Integrity Snatcher is like a warning sign—watch out for the people who empower your helplessness.

People who empower our helplessness are the ones who want us to think that we need them, that our life will not be the same without them, or that it will be better and more abundant with them. They say things like this:

- No one will ever love you like I love you.

- No one will ever make love to you like I do.

- Who else is always there for you when you need them?

- I taught you everything you know.

- Let me do it for you since only I can get it right.

- Only I can turn your book into a *New York Times* bestseller
  or help you make that project into a huge success.

It is their message, "You need me to . . ." be happy, loved, or success-ful that shakes our foundation and leaves us questioning if we can do it without them. They summon our voice of uncertainty and tap into our self-doubt. They dangle the bait of what we want most in front of us and leave us questioning if we can reach our goals and vision with-out them. In short, they hook into our deepest fears and empower our core feelings of helplessness! Even when that alarm inside goes off, and we feel the urge to walk or run away, the scared, insecure child inside of each of us who doesn't trust that we can do it on our own or that the Universe will provide becomes paralyzed and seduced into think-ing these people have something we don't. We end up giving away our power and allowing them to snatch our integrity.

✳

Integrity, like our power or even our greatness, can be like a hot potato. Not sure what to do with it, or thinking that life will be much harder if we have to own it or live it, we unknowingly try to avoid it. We try dropping it, stepping over it, or throwing it to someone else in the hope that they will catch it and make our life complete. If we are lucky, the person we throw it to will drop it or will throw it back. As I said, we can never eliminate all of our Integrity Snatchers, but hopefully, by understanding them, we will begin to recognize them for what they are—tricksters. They are the shame, fear, and stories that we made up when we were children because we did not understand what was going on or how to interpret the events in our life. Just as that little child needed love, love is what you need to bring to these Integrity Snatchers. When they start making noise and causing you to question your power, your abilities, and yourself, bring compassion to your fear, your shame, your shadows, your stories, your helpless victim, the part of you that *wants* so badly and can be seduced by someone who empowers helplessness. They need to be reassured that *everything* you need is inside of you.

That's what the next chapter is all about.

3 ## You Are the Only Expert on You!

We all have an inner voice. Some may call it gut instinct. Some may call it intuition. This inner voice recognizes what is best for us and is willing to speak to us if we are willing to listen.

Each of us has a different relationship to this voice. For some, it is a very close and trusting relationship. Others are hardly aware of its presence. Some people only hear their inner voice when they slow down long enough to pay attention. Others desperately want to hear it but cannot because of the constant chatter and incessant internal dialogue inside their head telling them, *Do this! No, do that! Don't do anything at all! Just do what everyone else is doing or what they tell you to do!*

When we don't listen to our inner voice, we look outside ourselves for guidance, even for our sense of self!

Think about it.

We buy things to get the approval of others. We accomplish milestones to get the respect of others. We become like gerbils on a never-ending wheel, running as fast as we can to do, have, or be all the "right" things, so others will accept us. We want to live in certain neighborhoods, drive a certain make and model of car, wear specific labels, belong to the right clubs or associations, hang around with certain people, have our children attend prestigious schools, and dine at the hottest restaurants, largely to affirm that we are "okay." Now, I am not saying that any of those things are "wrong" or "bad," especially if it is what you enjoy, has meaning to you, or puts a smile on your face!

Yet, trying to "keep up" automatically puts us behind because it comes from a place of lack! If you are pursuing things that the world tells you are valuable, you need to take a step back to decide if these things *truly* matter to you.

Anytime you are crafting your life to get the approval or validation of others, you will find yourself in trouble. It is simply unsustainable. Lily Tomlin famously said, "The trouble with the rat race is that even if you win, you're still a rat." It is a setup for disappointment, exhaustion, and the endless feeling that you are never quite enough. And I can promise you something: Even if you get all the things that you thought you wanted, one day, something will cause you to stop running. You will look at all the things you thought defined you and ask, *What was I running after? Why is my life filled with all these things that I don't even care about?*

It is a shocking and disturbing moment to discover you have spent your entire life chasing things that ultimately did not make you happy.

Living a life of integrity means you step out of that mindless rat race. You stop letting others tell you what you *should* want.

Take Back Your Power

Tracey had a crush on Jacob from the time she was in junior high school. He was the older brother of a girlfriend of hers. By the time they were in high school, they were dating, and everyone knew they would get married, which they did, right after college. They seemed to have the perfect suburban life: a beautiful son and daughter and a pet golden retriever. Yet after their children went away to college, it soon became obvious that Tracey and Jacob had grown apart and had little in common. Tracey wanted to travel, have adventures, and pursue a more spiritual path. Jacob was content staying home, watching sports on his big-screen TV, and playing golf on the weekends. The distance between them steamrolled into discontent, disagreements, and ultimately divorce—which was initiated by Tracey.

Everyone was shocked by this course of events. The children were particularly upset with Tracey for causing the upheaval. Anxious to escape all the tension and wanting to start anew, Tracey threw herself into her yoga practice. Venturing to different yoga studios in her area, Tracey met Steve. After seeing each other in class a few times and chatting on their way in and out of class, Steve asked Tracey if she wanted to get together. She said yes, and soon their connection was undeniable. They began spending all their free time together.

Steve was considerably younger than Tracey, yet she loved that he complemented her energy, had a zest for life, and shared her desire to go and explore new things. Steve had a much more modest life-style than Tracey, and that, combined with their age difference, caused Tracey to worry what her friends and family might think of the relationship. She tried to keep the relationship private. But as time went on, Steve was hurt by Tracey's insistence to keep her two lives separate. In his mind, if she was truly committed to the relationship, then it should no longer be a secret. They should merge their lives and let the world know that they were a serious couple.

Realizing she would lose him if she continued to keep him secret, Tracey agreed to introduce Steve to her friends and family. But soon, Tracey's fears were realized. Her friends had doubts, and in the name of "being a good friend," shared their concerns with Tracey. Her children wanted nothing to do with Steve. They thought their mother could and should find someone who was more her equal. They made it clear that Steve was not welcome at family dinners or holidays.

Tracey could not handle all the tension and fighting. She worried that her friends and family saw something she could not see in Steve, and she started pulling away. Steve was hurt and they agreed to take time apart to figure things out.

In a matter of days, Tracey was miserable. She missed Steve. She had never had a lover who was a best friend. After three weeks of feeling like this, Tracey decided that she could no longer let others dictate her truth. She called Steve and told him how she felt. She vowed to herself and to Steve that she would no longer compromise her happiness to please others. Tracey let her friends and children know how she felt. They did not need to like Steve, although she hoped they would give him a chance, but she would no longer tolerate any negative comments or questions about him.

Eventually everyone, even her children, started to see how happy Tracey was and were grateful that she had Steve in her life. Tracey couldn't believe the change. Because she stepped into her power and refused to allow others to dictate what was best for her, she had everything she had ever dreamed of.

Time to Stop "Shoulding" on Yourself

Many of us live with a long list of "shoulds." Our shoulds can be positive: *I should be the change I want to see in the world. I should do my part to take care of the planet.* Or like Tracey: *I should try to create peace and harmony in my family.* But there is often a dark side to our shoulds. Masters at manipulation, our shoulds push us to live in accordance with how *others* think we should be living. They can have us compromise our truth, disconnect from our vision, and overcommit to things that are not in alignment with our integrity. When it comes to describing shoulds, Debbie Ford said it best: "Our shoulds are nothing more than the continuation of what was; they are the cement that keeps us in the vicious cycle of drama and pain. Shoulds are like bloodsuckers and energy suckers, killing our chances for full self-expression. They are the nasty limitations that society throws at us each day and every day, the limitations that cut us off from the authentic choices of the higher aspect of ourselves and seal in our fate to live less than satisfying lives."[1]

When you understand that you are the only expert on you, you can take feedback from others while remembering to check in with your inner voice, your internal guidance system. Sure, Tracey's friends and family didn't like Steve. They thought she *should* be with someone older, more successful, more driven, more who-knows-what? But *she* knew he was the right person for her. While I'm sure their brief breakup was painful, that time apart gave Tracey the chance to truly hear her inner voice, and that was the only voice that mattered.

⚡ INTEGRITY INSIGHT

How are you "shoulding" on yourself? What do you tell yourself about the following topics?

- Where you should be in your life:
  By this stage of my life, I should have achieved . . .
- What your body should look like:
  I should be sexier, look younger, have thinner thighs, have six-pack abs . . .
- Your children:
  My kids should be more like . . .
- The qualities and emotions you possess:
  I should be smarter, more disciplined, happier, calmer, less angry . . .

What are your top five shoulds that cause you pain? If you stopped "shoulding" on yourself, how would you handle these situations?

A U-Turn Back to Yourself

To walk the path of integrity means that you must learn to trust that *you* are the one with all the answers. Instead of looking to the external world for truth, we need to make a U-turn back to ourselves, learn to go inward, and discover the voice that has been there all along. I call this the process of self-referral. It is a way of continually looking to yourself instead of the outer world for approval, answers, and guidance. Self-referral brings you back to you and empowers you. Deepak Chopra said, "It is an internal way of being that is not dependent on external circumstances."[2] You clear away the voices of society, friends, and family and determine what *you* like, what *you* care about, and what *your* priorities are in this lifetime. This allows you to access your authentic point of reference. This is your touchstone, your true essence, the part of you that knows what is best. It is the part of you not obscured by all the shoulds.

Although many spiritual teachers advocate learning to go inside, it can sometimes be tricky. Just like living inside of (ours or other people's) outdated stories of who we are can be an Integrity Snatcher, often our authentic point of reference gets clouded and confused by the voices of others. We have spent so much time being directed from outside that sometimes even when we think we are being guided by our authentic point of reference, it is actually the voice or desire of others. We have been living in accordance with that voice for so long that we think it is our own.

I see this all the time, especially with the millennials I work with. They have spent so much time trying to be the perfect son or daughter that they don't know where their parents' hopes and dreams for them end and their own begin. For example, one twenty-something came to me after having a knock-down, drag-out fight with his father.

It had always been assumed that Daniel would take over the family's real estate development business. After he finished college, he moved home and did just that. The deal was that he would learn the company from the ground up, starting by working as a construction worker. Daniel dutifully did what was expected of him. After eight months of feeling less than motivated and burnt out living someone else's life, he summoned the courage to tell his father that he was not sure that this was what he wanted to do with the rest of his life.

The truth was, Daniel had never even asked himself what he wanted to do with his life since it was always assumed that Daniel would take over the family empire. But as he feared, Daniel's father became enraged. He accused Daniel of being lazy and entitled. Daniel told me later that it felt like he was drowning in quicksand when he stood up to his father's wrath, but he stayed firm in his truth. He knew he needed to take a U-turn back to himself and find his passion. Otherwise, he could waste years or maybe his whole life pursuing something that was quite frankly wrong for him.

I'm not saying that living a life of integrity means you shirk responsibility. Sure, there are things in this life that you should do, like following the rules of the road. You can't avoid them. But we have lost touch with the fact that we are the co-creators of our lives. We are not helpless victims. We can check in and make sure what we are pursuing is what we truly want. And if it is not, there is always time to change lanes.

We can learn from Daniel's experience that the greater the force on the other side trying to influence your decision, the more challenging it feels to make that U-turn back to yourself. But when you can stand up to a parent or boss or lover and stay firm in what you know, you become even more certain, self-reliant, and self-referred.

⚡ INTEGRITY INSIGHT

Are you self-referred? Answer the following questions with yes or no:

1 Do you try to get people to perceive you in a certain way?

2 When you get an idea about how to improve some aspect of your life, are you more apt to start polling people for opinions rather than to just go with it?

3 Do you often say yes when you'd rather say no?

4 Is your home more of a reflection of your budget or of someone else's taste rather than a reflection of your personality?

5 Does guilt often affect your decision-making process?

6 Do you tend to define yourself in context to your relationship to someone else (I am X's wife, Y's best friend, Z's business partner)?

7 When it comes to making plans with your friends, is your first reaction to say, "I don't care what we do," or "You decide," or "Whatever you want"?

8 Do you often avoid expressing your needs and wants to your loved ones?

9 When you've been working around the clock and notice you're starting to fatigue, are you apt to keep drinking coffee instead of stopping to take a break?

10 In your family of origin, do you still tend to play the role you did when you were young because it is expected?

The more questions you answered with yes, the more you need to learn to be true to yourself!

The Ultimate Selfie Device

Whether you like to admit it or not, if you think back on most of the issues or crises you've faced in your life, there was likely a point in the unfolding of those events when you felt something was "off." Whether you actively and overtly played a part in creating the situation, like lying—even to yourself, or if your participation took the form of passivity or inaction—you ignored your inner knowing, you failed to set healthy boundaries, or you allowed the emotional baggage of past events to prevent you from doing something in the present—you were, in fact, a co-creator of the reality that you now deem problematic.

Remember, integrity is about saying goodbye to victimhood and hello to radical responsibility!

Maybe even right now you can identify an area in your life in which you are willfully ignoring, powerfully procrastinating about, or covering up something that doesn't feel right.

The good news is that we all have the most amazing GPS inside us to help us find our way back to what is right for us. That inner voice, that authentic point of reference, and the gift of self-referral, are all parts of your Integrity Alignment Monitor (the I AM). Your I AM is installed at birth and comes with a lifetime guarantee! In an era when we are all obsessed with selfies and self-monitoring—measuring every step we take, our sleeping patterns, the calories we consume or burn, the places we visit, and how much money we spend—our Integrity Alignment Monitor is truly the ultimate gadget or app because it connects us with ourselves. It supports us in knowing when something is "off." It warns us when we don't feel comfortable in someone's presence. It alerts us to behaviors, choices, thoughts, and actions that are not in alignment with our integrity, and it guides us in making the choices and decisions that are in our best interest.

Most of us have an inkling that this monitor is inside us, but the thought of having to continually check in with our I AM or be guided by it may feel daunting, as if we must strive to become a paragon of perfection or that it might be too hard, but living from your Integrity Alignment Monitor, this place of I AM, makes life easier. It is so much easier to live in alignment with and be authentic about who you are than to be a chameleon trying to please others. It's easier to make choices that are congruent with your truth and desires than it is to step over yourself, create some sort of implosion, and then have to clean up the mess you made, run damage control, take care of the drama, put out the fires, and start over at square one in order to get back on track.

Not only does your Integrity Alignment Monitor make life easier, but it is also easy to use. Simply tune in, ask, and listen. Your Integrity Alignment Monitor helps you connect with your gut feelings, your inner voice that tells you what's right for you and what's not. The Integrity Alignment Monitor will tell you how you are feeling. It is all about learning to say, "I AM . . ." and fill in the blank. *I am unhappy in this marriage. I am overweight. I am working too hard. I am scared of failing.* The Integrity Alignment Monitor helps us stand in who we are and own where we are at.

Most of us have not learned to use our I AM because we are so used to being outer referred or people pleasers. We have disconnected from our authentic point of reference—our own I AM—because we are always thinking, *Who or what do you want me to be?* The Integrity Alignment Monitor is the ultimate selfie device—not only does it help you *see* yourself, it helps you *be* yourself.

> Neale Donald Walsch said, "If you don't go within, you go without."[3] I'd add, when you go within, you never have to go without!

We all are emotional beings. Learning to say I AM means we can connect within and determine how we are feeling. Our emotions are an important part of our internal guidance system. Yet many people have no clue what they're feeling or experiencing at any given moment. When you ask them, "How are you?" they automatically reply, "Fine" or "Fabulous" or "Hanging in there" or "I am alive" or "Everything is status quo." Or perhaps as is common nowadays: "Busy! But good!" Generally, this robotic and flat-lined state of being was programmed during our youth. Many of us learned to become numb to our feelings because of being told "You should be seen and not heard" or "Stop crying, or I will give you something to cry about" or "You are too sensitive" or "Big boys or girls don't cry" or "People won't like you if you are angry, so put on a happy face." Some of us were not only told to stop crying but to stop laughing, too, since any sort of noise or emotion was discouraged. If we lived in an atmosphere where we were told, "There's no such thing as happiness!" chances are that we detached from our positive emotions as well as our negative ones.

To live a life of integrity, we must develop a healthy and trusting relationship with our emotions. (One of the steps in part 2 will support you in doing just that.) To tune in to our Integrity Alignment Monitor, we have to understand that our emotions are here to educate us. They are here to guide us and inform us. So instead of making them "wrong," suppressing them, or trying to fix them, we should be fascinated by them. We should see them as a red flag that is waving and alerting us to *Come here! Look here. There is something I need to show you, something you need to see.*

However, since our Integrity Alignment Monitors do not come in a cool box and with an instruction manual, I'll share some key characteristics of integrity that are important to keep in mind as you learn to tune back in to your I AM.

Integrity Is Personal

What might be in agreement with one person's Integrity Alignment Monitor may not be in agreement with another's. We can sometimes get very righteous about what integrity is or is not. We've got to remember that it's personal. Don't use integrity as a righteous sword to belittle others. We don't know what is right for anyone else, just like they don't know what is right for us. Stay focused on yourself!

Integrity Is a Fluid Concept

Since as humans we are always evolving, what was in integrity for us last year, month, or week may not be in integrity with who we are or what we desire today. For years, I did not speak with a friend I had a falling out with. I would avoid her because it felt out of integrity for me to pretend to kiss her on the cheek or make small talk. A few years ago, that changed. The concept of continuing to avoid her or lug around some story from the past felt cumbersome and exhausting. It felt more out of integrity with who I had become to hold on to this resentment. I texted her and we spoke. Knowing that integrity is fluid, I could tune in to my I AM, recalibrate the settings, and honor my new direction based on what was right for me in that moment.

Integrity Is Area Specific

We may be very skilled at living in integrity in one area of our life and completely out of touch with our integrity in another. And that's okay. But what we also need to understand is that integrity isn't a one-size-fits-all scenario. What is right for us in one area of our life might not fit the other areas. For example, regarding finances, our I AM might be guided by "play it safe." However, maybe in other areas of our life, like pursuing our passion or in our social life, "playing it safe" may be what is out of integrity for us because it keeps us playing small.

When I first got divorced and was a single mom, I realized that I couldn't do it all, and even if I could, I had to set my priorities, or I might be in constant turmoil deciding what came first. When I started to date, inevitably I would get halfway to wherever I was going, the phone would ring, and it would be one of my daughters—they needed advice or were upset about something. At first, I tried to work it out, to continue on my way and try to talk them through whatever issues they were facing. I tried to convince myself that it would be okay, that they needed to learn empowering skills or coping mechanisms. But they had gone through tremendous change, and they needed to know that they were always my top priority. When it came to my children, my motto was, "They come first. No exceptions." My I AM was set to that, and it made decisions quite easy because I always followed that directive. In other areas of my life, I would be more apt to consider each situation on an "as come" basis. For example, maybe I would cancel a workout if I needed to do something else. Living by the motto "No exceptions" when it came to exercise felt out of integrity. It is important that you set your Integrity Alignment Monitor not only in relation to the different areas of your life, but also in alliance with the priorities of those areas of your life.

Integrity Is Black and White

There is no gray area—your Integrity Alignment Monitor *knows* when something is off. You are either in or out of integrity—there is no "kind of" in or "a little bit" out.

Integrity Gets Stronger with Use

Our Integrity Alignment Monitors are like watches that wind automatically and grow stronger and last longer with use. The more you tune in to your I AM, the better it functions. The more you become present to the actions, reactions, inactions, behaviors, patterns, and thoughts that lead you further in or out of integrity, the sharper your I AM will be, and the easier your life will become. You will know instantly whether something will or will not serve your highest self so that you can avoid any potholes that may be in your path and cause you to fall!

Integrity Is Not about Perfection

I know that some people may not even want to pick up this book because the word *integrity* can be intimidating—way too high of a standard and not a fun or sexy way to live your life. But living a life of integrity does not mean that you need to become some paragon of perfection. It is more about choosing to live on a level of consciousness where you are aware, responsible, and thoughtful about your choices. I can be committed to healthy eating and still have pizza or three bites of chocolate molten lava cake and not make myself "wrong." I can make the decision to play hooky from work, not look at my computer all weekend, or spend an afternoon under the covers watching old movies and not feel remorse. The difference is that I am consciously making choices and using my I AM to make sure that my choices feel good to me. The benefit of this is that I no longer beat myself up for anything after the fact and no longer spend precious time wishing I had done things differently. By taking the time to consult your I AM before you act, you get to determine what is "perfect" for you in the moment.

Be Fascinated

Most of us have been taught that for every situation there is an end game, a destination we want to reach. Completion is important. It is healthy, inspiring, and feeds our internal flame to claim the moment, stop and feel gratitude, bask in our accomplishments, and celebrate ourselves and life. Success breeds success, and that sense of completion, celebration, and acknowledgment becomes the motivation for what comes next.

The thing is, integrity is not an end game; it is an evolution.

Life is not static. Transformation is not linear and integrity is a dynamic way of being. There is no completion, only the opportunity to take our next evolutionary leap.

The Integrity Advantage is about constantly being fascinated with life, being curious about what we are experiencing and ultimately what we could be learning.

✳

Recognize that your growth is a continual process, your ceiling becoming your new floor as you keep moving upward in your integrity. *Be excited when you find your next integrity issue since that will be your next big breakthrough.* To some, this way of life may at first sound exhausting, but once you commit to the practice, you will see that there is no better way to live life. Your actions and choices will all be sourced from a place of fullness, guided by what is in your highest integrity, leaving little room for self-doubt, indecision, and self-sabotage. Believe me when I say . . .

Integrity is the new easy!

4

If You Always Do What You've Always Done, You'll Always Get What You've Always Gotten

As humans, we don't recognize how powerful we are.

The Integrity Advantage is about reclaiming that power and using it to get what we truly want.

Whether we realize it or not, at every moment we are co-creating our life. Perhaps you acknowledge that you co-create your life by the choices you make and actions you undertake or don't: *Accept the job or say no? Break up or get married?* But we are not always present to the fact that we also create our life with every thought and belief we have. So not only do we create our life, but we also *call it forth* through our thoughts and beliefs. It is our unconscious mind (which experts say is perhaps as much as 90 percent more powerful than our conscious mind) that is the source of most of our thoughts, beliefs, and commitments. Bottom line—our unconscious shapes who we are and what we do!

We each have an internal blueprint deep within our psyche, under our conscious awareness, that calls forth our life. Our soul is designed to evolve, and that is always its goal. Every person and situation is part of our evolutionary process: a lesson to be learned, a gift waiting to be opened, so we can heal the wounds of our past. *The Universe is our most benevolent teacher, friend, and partner when it comes to supporting our growth.* It is always serving up the situation, putting the perfect person right in front of us, and pointing us in the direction of what needs to be addressed so that we can unravel whatever is going on and gain access to the insight that will catapult us into the next version of who we are meant to become. And if we miss the messages, it will keep bringing forth similar situations. The Universe is trying to get us to wake up and heal, so we can make different choices. It is yelling at us. But we are often deaf to its calls.

That is, until things get *painfully obvious*.

I often say that people don't seek me out when their life is terrific. They wait until the sadness, anger, hurt, frustration, or resignation become so profound that they cannot bear it anymore. Although it would be nice to think that people can learn from joy, pain is the great motivator of change. And the Universe uses pain as a form of feedback.

What do you think of when you hear the word *feedback*? Most of us equate feedback with criticism. We picture a disapproving look from an upset parent, a stern elementary school teacher, a disappointed employer, a troubled friend, or an angry spouse. But feedback isn't always something that comes from a person. I'll show you how you can get feedback from situations, relationships, and even your body. These are different ways the Universe is trying to wake you up and bring you back into integrity. When you see it as the source of useful information, feedback—whether positive or negative—can have a profound influence on your life. It is then that you truly accept the Universe as a kind and benevolent teacher.

Situational Feedback

The Universe is always providing us with the experiences, challenges, and lessons that become the foundation for our next insight or piece of wisdom. Often we don't realize that everything is happening "for us" and not "to us." As we've seen, we are programmed to slip into the role of the victim, the "poor me, it's unfair" mentality, and believe that life is conspiring against us, but the truth is, it is working *with* us! There is no question that life sometimes is unfair and does hurt, but every challenge we encounter is an opportunity to grow and learn. And if you are standing in the power that you are the co-creator of your life, then you know that you called in that situation, challenge, or person because your soul knew that you needed that experience, exactly as it was—tumultuous or easy, heartbreaking or heart opening, positive or negative—to further your evolution.

Most people miss the message because they are not seeing themselves as a co-creator. They are not asking themselves questions like these:

- What am I supposed to be learning from the embarrassment of being humiliated by my spouse/friend/teenager/boss?

- Why did I have to endure yet another broken heart?

- What is the Universe trying to show me by all the drama I am experiencing in so many of the areas of my life?

I know that if I am experiencing chaos in my outer world, if in the span of two days I have lost my sunglasses, misplaced my keys, gotten a traffic ticket, run late for appointment after appointment, dropped my cellphone in the toilet, and spilled water on my computer, that is a message from the Universe that something inside me is off. There is internal chaos that is creating chaos in my outer world. The internal chaos might be that I am not feeding some unmet need, lack structure, or need a break. But whatever it is, I am always looking at the situations in my life and trying to uncover what they are trying to teach me.

This frame of reference can change everything. When we no longer see a situation as happening to us, but instead as happening *for* us, we can begin to look inside, to see what needs to be dealt with.

Relational Feedback

Not only does the Universe give us feedback in the form of situations that are meant to deliver messages, but it also sends us messengers. Our relationships, especially those people closest to us, serve as our strongest mirrors and greatest guides. They are there to show us the parts of ourselves that we have disowned, hidden from ourselves, lost, or that need to be healed.

We often hear transformational teachers say, "There's no one out there." When we are in relationship with others, we tend to make it all about them. We think about what *they* did wrong, how *their* behavior was inappropriate, and what *they* could or should be doing differently. It's not about them. The people in our life are there to act as reflections—to illuminate the shadows we need to own, the wounds we need to heal, and the outdated beliefs we need to reveal and shift so that we can be our fullest and most loving selves.

Even the people who break our hearts come bearing a gift. Their presence in our life and all that transpires occur to give us the opportunity to gain new insight, so our soul can evolve. When most of us get hurt by a breakup or experience pain from a relationship, we don't automatically think, *Wow! How lucky I am that I got my heart broken.* Instead, we tend to blame the other person or beat ourselves up. We think, *If only I was smarter, better looking, in better shape, more successful, sensual, or spontaneous—then maybe things would not have happened as they did. Maybe he or she would not have left or found someone else.* Although it might hurt—and believe me, I have been there and know that it can leave you breathless—consider the following questions:

- What if their leaving was the best thing that could have ever happened to you?

- What if their leaving had nothing to do with you?

- What if that one more broken heart was what your soul needed so that you could do the work and create the insight and opening to finally find the love of your life?

If there is no one out there, then on one hand, their leaving, cheating, or doing whatever they did had to do with their own wounds and the opportunity to discover what they needed to learn in this lifetime. And on the other hand, their leaving, cheating, or doing whatever they did was totally for *you* in that it gave you the invitation to see what you were projecting onto them or the relationship, so you could own back that light or dark and more fully embrace all of yourself. It also served as the catalyst to rip the bandage off a wound from the past, so it could finally be examined and healed, allowing you to love more deeply.

I know this firsthand. As I was trying to recover from the pain of my divorce, I had to ask, *Why did I call forth this kind of man and this kind of tumultuous relationship?* Knowing that my soul drew it in for a reason, what was I meant to be learning?

Well of course, lesson number one was that I knew I had stepped over my truth and ignored all the signs, preferring to keep on track with my to-do list of life.

I also knew that I had followed my head, but lesson number two was how disconnected I was from my heart. It had never occurred to me that it was a place I could look for answers.

Have you ever heard the expression "If you spot it, you got it"? It essentially is talking about projection—it means that anything you see in others is within yourself. To get my next list of lessons, I had to look deep inside myself. *How was I like my ex-husband?* I had to dare to name all those things I judged in him, so I could see those very things in myself.

Like many newly divorced people, I had a list of his flaws! But when I looked at all the things that had frustrated me, caused me pain, made me feel the fool, it all boiled down to one thing: I could not trust him.

There it was. I knew I had to deal with it and uncover how and why I called it forth. *Why did I need to experience a situation fraught with so many trust issues? What were my beliefs about trust? What were the messages I received as a child that were embedded into my unconscious and internal operating system?*

I thought back to my childhood. I was taught, "You can't trust anyone." You can't trust your friends—they will gossip behind your back. You can't trust others with your possessions—they will ruin or not return them. You can't trust therapists—they will tell the world your problems. You can't even trust those you love—they will betray and hurt you.

In reaction to these messages, I became Miss Loyal, Miss Perfect, Miss My-Word-Is-My-Bond. I hadn't healed my trust issues; I'd created a persona over them.

My unconscious belief, "You can't trust anyone," had become my self-fulfilling prophecy.

As part of my shadow work, I examined how I might have been untrustworthy. Like everyone, I gossiped and let people down at times, but where I was truly untrustworthy was when it came to myself. I kept stepping over my truth, compromising, biting my tongue, and swallowing my integrity.

The Universe had been shouting at me for years, trying to wake me up. *Kelley, you've got some healing to do.* It wasn't until the struggle of my marriage that the Universe got my attention—the pain was too great! Yet, the good news is that only a person with trust issues would write a book about integrity! Those issues, that relationship, that pain, led me here—to my life's work.

What about you? Where do you experience pain in your relationships? Our partners, family, and friends are always providing us feedback about which qualities we have disowned. Anytime we are triggered by another person, we need to determine which quality that person is displaying that is setting us off. Is it their selfishness, laziness, or stupidity? Their tendency to lie, judge, be negative, or control? It's like finding the clues on a treasure map—uncovering that which you reject in yourself is your road map back to wholeness! What you can't stand in others is something that needs to be healed in you.

Not only do our relationships provide feedback about the negative qualities that we have disowned but the positive ones as well. When we are awestruck by a quality we see in another—bowled over by their brilliance and bravery, captivated by their creativity and charisma, mesmerized by their magnificence and motivation, or silenced by their spontaneity and sexiness—they are holding up a mirror reflecting the parts of ourselves that we need or want to embrace. Even when we fall in love, we are generally connecting with the parts of ourselves that we don't see in ourselves. Once again, the Universe is our ally. Always acting in real time, it continually reflects the quality that we need to own in that moment to evolve or accomplish our next goal. When we transfer our light onto somebody else, it takes away our access to it, and we cannot be as successful or grand as we would have been if we had access to and were fully able to express that quality in the world. It's like missing a secret ingredient in a recipe—the result might still turn out okay, but the secret ingredient is what would make it delicious.

Put aside the idea that our relationships are meant for "happily ever after." Some may be and others not, but they all support our wholeness. Understanding projection opens us to realizing that everything in the outer world is within us. It supports us in becoming our fullest expression of self and embracing all we are. As we fall more in love with more parts of ourselves, not only does self-love expand, but so does our ability to love others.

Body Feedback

The third and the most powerful way the Universe attempts to wake us up is through our bodies—it is the one messenger that we ultimately cannot ignore. Our bodies are always giving us feedback on how we are managing our life as well as what lessons we need to learn. They always let us know how and if we are taking enough care of our life, but we tend to ignore the messages.

I meet so many people who are not taking care of their body. They work too much, take on too much stress, don't eat or sleep well, or are somehow out of balance. Their body tries to tell them that they are out of whack—they catch a cold, have headaches, fall asleep during a conference call, or trip when rushing to their car. Yet we still don't listen, we keep living life in the same manner. Our body keeps trying—maybe the cold becomes a flu, the headaches become migraines, or the next stumble results in a broken bone. And, we *still* don't listen! It's like the Universe knocks and knocks, and when we continue not to hear the calling, it has no choice but to do something, sometimes drastic, to get our attention. It has no choice but to smash down our door.

This happened to me when I was mentally exhausted from ping-ponging back and forth about my marriage—*Do I stay, or should I go?* Trying to make the relationship work was like pushing a boulder up a hill, but because I have always been the "strong one," I kept pushing. Too arrogant to think that my body would ever betray me, I was shocked when I fainted at a social gathering! That's when I knew my body wasn't giving out on me, but instead was sending me the wake-up call I couldn't ignore!

Remarkably, there is often a direct correlation between our physical issues and the insight we need to realize. For example, the person with a stiff neck needs to stop looking back at the past. The person with constant headaches needs to look at the incessant negative internal dialogue that keeps looping around in their mind. The person with leg issues needs to look at how they are stuck and unable to move forward.

Susan's body taught her one of her greatest lessons: how to be alone. Susan grew up in the house that all the kids wanted to go to. The smell of freshly baked cookies welcomed them at the door, and Susan's kind and upbeat parents made it so no child ever wanted to leave. She was always surrounded by love and laughter. She met Bruce while she was in college and basically went from her parents' home to the home she made with her husband, never once being on her own.

Susan and Bruce were married for twenty-five years and led a very full life. They had two children and a huge circle of friends. Bruce, who was a visionary with an entrepreneurial spirit, was a big presence in the community. Their home became the place where their kids' friends congregated as well as the epicenter for many huge parties, political fundraisers, and charitable events. Susan thrived when she was surrounded by people.

One day, it was as if the music suddenly stopped! Bruce left. Susan's mother died of cancer. Her two children went away to school. Eventually, she even moved out of the family home. The loss was enormous, as was Susan's fear of being alone.

Susan realized that she needed to take the time to reflect, grieve, and heal, and she did, but always in the company of her women's group, therapist, or friends. Although she knew that the Universe was giving her the opportunity to learn to be by herself, she could not bear it—the silence was too loud. So Susan did what she always did—she kept busy and surrounded herself with people. She not only had one plan per night, she always had a backup plan or two, just in case! She never went out alone, but always had a friend or companion with her. Susan was not concerned if he was Mr. Right or Mr. Wrong, as long as he was right there right now.

Although the Universe gave her several opportunities to get to know herself and own her power in a whole new way, the one invitation that Susan would not accept was the one to be alone or to slow down.

This went on for about eight years. Then, as tends to happen when we are not paying attention to what the Universe is trying to teach us, the Universe literally knocked her down. It was the day after her son's engagement party, which had taken place in her former home where Bruce now lived with his new wife. Susan went Rollerblading to try to work out some of the emotion that had arisen because of the party, and she took a terrible fall. She pinched a nerve in her neck and developed trigeminal neuralgia, which is a pain in the facial muscles that is considered one of the most painful afflictions known to medical practitioners. There was no pill strong enough and no therapy potent enough to lessen her excruciating pain. Although she did everything she could, when she wasn't at therapy or with a doctor or healer, Susan spent her time in bed, lights off, covered with heating pads. She couldn't speak or move, and she did not want company. As the pain subsided, she could do a bit more. Still needing to be gentle with herself, she started listening to music, reading books, and watching TV. Little by little, she started appreciating getting to choose what she wanted to watch, read, or listen to without having to consider anyone else.

Susan recovered and was thrilled when several months later she could dance at her other son's wedding. She still had a bit more to learn—the day after the wedding, she was playing golf and *whack!* The pain returned! Susan knew that if she wanted to regain her quality of life, she would need surgery.

Her recovery from spinal surgery was like graduate school when it came to getting her education in being alone. She learned to love her own company more each day. Susan now understands the rhythm of life and loves her alone time—she is vehement about claiming and protecting it. Although pain was the *impetus* for Susan's healing, the recovery and transformation came when she learned to be alone.

Here's the bottom line: when it comes to our body, if we don't listen to it, it won't listen to us!

*

Our outer world holds up a mirror, an invitation to look within. It gives us an opportunity to see how we need to change and grow. *As we shift our inner world, the outer world will follow.* Understanding the magnitude of this reciprocal relationship of the outer and the inner—how the outer is always reflecting to us what is going on inside us—is a huge advantage when we commit to an integrity-guided life. We only need to remember to look in that mirror to see where we're stuck, experiencing chaos, making unhealthy choices, or not creating what we say we want. That is our signal to look inside, to see what is going on. As you tend to your inner world, your outer world will follow. This will enable us to leave bad relationships, break lazy habits, and embrace positive structure and actions. We'll see opportunity where we never did before. If we don't look in that mirror, we'll continue to do what we've always done and get what we've always gotten.

When you experience the gift of feedback, you'll realize how often you've been settling and how costly mediocrity can be.

INTEGRITY INSIGHT

What in your life is painfully obvious?

- Is there a situation that is causing you frustration or angst? *If you see that situation as a mirror, what is it trying to reveal to you?*
- Is there a relationship in your life that triggers you or causes pain? *Why is this person in your life? What are they there to show or teach you? What disowned quality do you project onto them that you need to take back?*
- Is there any "dis-ease" in your body or issue with your health? *What is it trying to show you? If the "dis-ease" in your body is a metaphor for or directly correlated to some insight you are supposed to see about your life, what is that?*
- How does your outer world reflect your inner world? *What do you see? What is the state of your union?*

5 The Intolerance of Mediocrity

I love that integrity can't be fooled. We can lie to ourselves, be in denial, or avoid things, but integrity is integrity—it is black or white. When we're out of alignment, it shows up. It may show up in our body or relationships, with money or work, or it may show up in multiple areas simultaneously. The Universe will reflect integrity back at us and give us the opportunity to regain balance. The more connected we are to our Integrity Alignment Monitor, the faster we'll know or feel when we are out of integrity, and the clearer and more certain we will be about what we need to do next because, *ultimately, all the integrity issues we have are with ourselves.*

As we experience the advantages that come with living in integrity, we'll never want to go back. When I stepped away from my marriage, finally owning it wasn't the right relationship for me, my eyes opened to all the other areas of my life where I was settling. I vowed I would no longer tolerate mediocrity in my love life, in my career, in my friendships, or with my health.

Some people may think that intolerance is a negative trait or a quality that should not be displayed, but *intolerance is a tap on the shoulder from your most magnificent self, trying to awaken you to your true potential.* When you look back at history, you will find that all social change and movements for justice and equality were sparked by a person's or group's intolerance of the status quo. The same is true of intolerance on a personal level. Choosing not to accept my own mediocrity was the emotional push I needed. It gave me the inspiration to take radical responsibility for where I was in each area of my life, so I could get to where I wanted to be.

We don't even realize how often we settle for crumbs. Trying to convince ourselves that our nice little life is enough, even if we don't feel authentically alive. Most people do not own what is possible for them. They focus on surviving instead of thriving. They commit to ordinary instead of even considering extraordinary. Although settling for "good enough" might feel safe, it is not. It compromises our opportunities for mental or spiritual growth, fosters stagnation, and casts us in the role of victim.

Taking ownership of our magnificence is a powerful demarcation point. It is a declaration that enough is enough, and we are ready to step into a new level of consciousness and commitment. It is a declaration that we are no longer willing to play safe and small and tolerate mediocrity; our birthright is to live our greatest desires.

Inaction is a common barrier for so many people—most of us would rather not rock the boat or take a risk, choosing instead to repeat mistakes and continue to live out of our integrity. This inaction takes many forms, including procrastination, denial, failing to speak out, and as with my journey, settling for mediocrity. Not only are these types of self-sabotaging behaviors an impediment toward living in our integrity, but when we engage in choices and actions that are not in line with what we truly want, feelings of unworthiness emerge—playing small makes us feel small. Those feelings of unworthiness, in turn, reinforce inaction. Even though it may sound counterintuitive, our egos engage in acts of self-sabotage to prove how unworthy we believe ourselves to be. After all, if we don't own who we are and what we deserve, and value ourselves enough to aim a little higher, it's hard to rationalize crawling out from under the cozy, familiar blanket of "good enough."

⚡ INTEGRITY INSIGHT

What are the situations or aspects of your life that you can no longer tolerate?

- Where do you settle, play small, accept crumbs, or stick to old patterns?
- Where have you been tolerating more than you should?
- Are you telling yourself a situation is fine or bearable, "okay for now," when it truly is not?

Are You Finally Fed Up with Being Fed Up?

I hear so many stories from people who can't get out of their own way. They are trapped in the cycle of losing and gaining the same twenty pounds, juggling the same cash crisis, looking for passion in a dead-end situation, or searching for their soulmate in all the wrong places. They have long-winded explanations for why X, Y, or Z hasn't happened. Yet underneath their litany of justifications, stories of limitation, and excuses lay resignation and fear. Unfortunately, they have lost trust in themselves and the benevolence of the Universe. The reality is, it only takes one area of unrest in your life to ruin your life!

We all have the power to create more passionately, to love more deeply, to experience more joyfully, and to reach our full potential. We need to reach that point of being fed up with being fed up. We know pain is the great motivator for transformation, yet so is intolerance of our mediocrity. It can catapult us from inertia to action and from stagnation to stupendous. When we can no longer tolerate our own excuses, patterns of procrastination, or drama, change can happen. When we are finally willing to be straight with ourselves and accept that we're settling for mediocre by listening to the voice that tells us to play small, be safe, and sell out, we've taken the first step to creating a new future.

Getting back into integrity begins with tapping into our intolerance and stamping out fear. Then, it's a matter of reconnection—healing that wound of trust with ourselves, others, and the powers of the Universe that are always there to support us.

From Fear to Faith to Freedom

When we believe that we are alone, that we are a separate being, and no one or nothing is guiding us or supporting us, we render ourselves out of integrity with all that we are and all that is possible. We have disconnected from the whispers of our soul and the magic of the Universe. Closed off and shut down, we become limited to a smaller sense of self and smaller levels of opportunities. Our human mind can only fathom a certain number of possibilities, but when we connect to the divinity of the Universe, we pair with a powerful partner, and the possibilities are endless.

"Being connected" is not about religion or God, and it is not about any one spiritual practice. Being connected is about recognizing both our grandeur and smallness, our humanity and divinity. It is about understanding that to be in integrity, not only do we need to connect to the wholeness of who we are, but also be plugged into the knowledge that something bigger than you or me is always supporting us. We are in a synchronistic relationship with the Universe, and consequently, we always have the most powerful partner by our side, supporting us as we step out of the smallness of our fears and tolerance of our limitations and into the reality of our hopes and desires. Faith is an essential ingredient in a life of integrity, giving us courage, confidence, and certainty to own all of who we are. It is the bridge between mediocrity and magnificence, fear and freedom.

My youngest daughter, Ryann, is someone who lives with a great sense of faith and connection. When she was in high school, she decided that she wanted to be an actress, and her dream was to attend the Bachelor of Fine Arts program at the University of Southern California. This is a highly competitive program. Thousands apply from around the globe, and only sixteen students are admitted, half of them female.

The students who apply for these coveted spots all have top grades and scores and resumes full of impressive acting experiences. Ryann had good grades, but she was not top of her class. Unlike many applicants, she lacked a resume of acting experiences. In fact, she had hardly ever been in a school play and was never a lead. Her desire to become an actress was born out of her love of watching television and becoming totally transfixed by a story. Attending a summer program in acting at USC cemented her desire to go there, but even with that, it was without question a long shot that she would be accepted into the program.

Ryann applied to only four colleges. A week before USC sent its decision letters, she found out that she did not get into her second choice college, which by all accounts was a much easier school to get into. The night she received this disappointing news, I happened to be out for the evening. She called me, crying hysterically. She was devastated. I came home immediately, but she refused to talk about it. She knew what we were all thinking: *If you didn't get into your second choice, how could you possibly get into USC?* Yet no one was allowed to ask that question. Ryann forbade it!

Being a mother who likes to plan, and wanting to soften the inevitable blow of rejection, I tried to talk to her about going to her safety school, where she had already been accepted. She refused to engage in this discussion or any discussion about a plan B. She believed she belonged in the BFA program at USC and would not let anyone shake her conviction. We hardly spoke for a week. Our only thoughts were about college, a topic we could no longer discuss. I cringed when I saw her wearing her USC T-shirt to bed. My biggest fear was not that she wouldn't get into USC, but that if she didn't, she would disconnect, lose confidence in her faith, and stop living from her strong sense of what was right for her. She was trying to live in a place of integrity. I begged the Universe to help Ryann deal with what I was sure would be disappointment.

On April 1—yes, April Fool's Day—the letter arrived from USC. It also happened to be Ryann's eighteenth birthday, so the magnitude of its arrival on this auspicious day was profound. I was in my home office and on the phone with a client when I heard yelling. I never hang up on clients, but this was an exception!

I ran out of my office. Ryann was standing on the stairs, letter in hand, hysterically crying. She had gotten into the BFA program at USC! Tears streamed down both of our faces as we embraced. My daughter had taught me the power of faith. She is an example of what is possible when you are in integrity with the Universe—when you know something in the core of your being, are in total alignment with your highest truth, and stand in the conviction that the Universe is there to support you.

⚡ INTEGRITY INSIGHT

- On a scale of 1 to 10, with 1 being "nonexistent" and 10 being "without doubt," where is your faith in the Universe?
- What belief stands in the way of you feeling more connected and cultivating more faith?
- What is the thought you need to affirm to truly stand in faith and open to opportunities of this synchronistic relationship with the Universe?
- What would be possible if you tapped into this powerful partnership?

Are You Ready?

Choosing to live in integrity is a declaration to the Universe and to all of those around you that you are finally ready to own all of who you are—that you are a powerful co-creator, that you are worthy and deserving to live the life you were meant to live, that you are complete. Once you own your greatness, a whole new vision of what is possible emerges.

The next part of this book will walk you through a process of digging deeper and identifying where and how you are out of integrity in your life. You will dismantle all the ways you've been trying to cover up this breach—the stories, the personas, the self-sabotage. You will clear the shoulds that have been obstructing you your entire life. Then, you will be able to move forward, ready to create life on your own terms, always knowing that you have the power to connect to your integrity anytime to determine whether you are on the right path. As Glinda the Good Witch said to Dorothy in *The Wizard of Oz*, "You've always had the power." She was right. When you live an integrity-guided life, you too have the power—all you have to do is take that U-turn back to yourself and find your way home.

part 2
THE INTEGRITY PROCESS

6

STEP ONE Get Naked

No, the first step in the Integrity Process isn't being an exhibitionist. It's about facing the truth. It's about revealing what you've been covering up for so long. It's time to strip down, peel off the layers of protection, and break through the illusions that obscure the truth of what's going on. It is a moment of courage, of downright bravery, when you decide to take a hard look at what has been holding you back.

It's time for radical honesty.

One of the things that made Debbie Ford so special was her tell-it-like-it-is personality. Knowing that "it is your secrets that make you sick," she was authentic and transparent about her own life. In candidly sharing her experiences, she led by example and gave others permission to do the same. She was always willing to bust herself, and people trusted her because of this. They looked forward to her brutal honesty. I, too, have been known to be "compassionately ruthless." And I think this trait, as well as my desire to always dig deeper, was among the reasons Debbie trusted me to continue her work.

I want to help people, not hurt them. If you don't want to remain stuck or in pain, what good does a *little* honesty do? Remember, people don't work with coaches, attend workshops, have sessions with healers, psychics, and astrologers, or shop in the self-help section of a bookstore if everything in their life is wonderful. That gnawing feeling that you are meant for something more is the impetus for change. The good news is that *suffering is optional.* We do not need to stay in our pain, frustration, discontent, or struggle. Yet, the only way out is *through*! If a wound is going to heal, if change is going to happen, then the bandage that you have worn for years that is "holding things together" needs to be ripped off!

The first step in the Integrity Process is radical and total honesty. It is time to operate in reality rather than continue to live in the trance of denial.

Take off the Blinders!

No matter how honest we think we are being with ourselves, we all have blind spots. There is a saying, "The only person in a room that can't see you, is you!" Think of the times when you didn't realize that you had gained ten pounds, couldn't admit that a relationship was no longer working, didn't want to face that your child had an issue, or tried to avoid admitting how angry you were. These are blind spots, things we would avoid looking at even if we were standing in front of a three-way mirror.

In 2002, when I first started training to be an Integrative Life Coach, part of the training included working through the material I would eventually be using to coach others. Each time I went through the experience of being coached, I had to choose two areas of my life that weren't working or that I wanted to improve. During the yearlong training, I tackled my body image and losing weight, my career and finding my purpose, becoming more financially responsible, cleaning out the clutter in my home, and creating more balance in my life. I worked through many areas of my life, but still I had a big hole of unhappiness. I finally shared this truth with a close friend, and her only comment was, "Well, Kelley, you have addressed everything except the elephant in the room."

The elephant in the room was my marriage. I had spent a year actively examining and transforming the areas of my life that were causing me feelings of discontent, but I had skipped the area that was so *painfully obvious* to everyone else. *I was blinded by my blind spot!* My friend's comment woke me up. It was my catalyst to acknowledge the sadness, resignation, and disappointment I felt about my marriage.

It was time for radical honesty.

Humans are very smart creatures. From early on, we find ways to avoid our blind spots, keep safe, and manage or control life so that we don't have to feel unwanted emotions, experience negative circumstances, or deal with what we perceive to be painful situations—from the child who learns to turn on the TV or hide in their room so they don't have to hear their parents fight, to me, a twenty-seven-year-old woman turning away from problems in my courtship and marriage. Not wanting to face the unfaceable, we are all pros at turning a blind eye.

Often, overlooking our blind spots comes in the form of denial.

It might happen like this: You find lipstick on your spouse's shirt or Viagra hidden in the back of his drawer. Your I AM starts going off. "I AM worried," it says. "Something is going on." And yet you throw the shirt in the wash or close the drawer. You bury the knowledge that has arisen. You don't want to have to deal with the truth.

Or people are getting laid off and there are significant budget cuts at work. Your boss tells you everything is fine with the business, and you choose to believe her, even though you can see that there are problems.

Or my trick: never look in a full-length mirror. When I was younger, I would only look at my face. Not my body. And I *never* looked at my whole body naked.

You may have heard the acronym for DENIAL:

Don't
Even
Notice
I
Am
Lying

We think that ignoring the truth protects us from it. But it's our resistance to the truth, our resistance to what *is*, that is the glue that keeps us stuck and in pain. Denial seems like a clever place to hide. It keeps us anchored in a seemingly safe harbor where everything is familiar. It may be a mess, but at least it feels familiar! When sheltered by denial, we often interpret threats and problems as benign or pretend that they don't exist. Like all blind spots, we can't see through our denial. It's insidious. But if we are going to live lives of integrity, we must confront our denial. We must recognize that denial keeps us blind to what *is* and limits our ability to find positive solutions and inspiring possibilities.

We're all masters of self-deception and self-indulgence, and the thing I find fascinating is that whether we realize it or not, we fight to hold on to our denial. We ignore the writing on the wall. We tell ourselves lies about how things will get better or change on their own, even though we know they will not. We cling to our righteousness instead of considering that there might be a better way. We put on rose-colored glasses, even when we know they obstruct us from seeing clearly. It is time to take it all off! But before we can, we must become aware of the clever ways we indulge our denial.

DENIAL INDULGER 1   Wishful Thinking

Wikipedia defines wishful thinking as "the formation of beliefs and making decisions based on what might be pleasing to imagine instead of by appealing to evidence, rationality, or reality."[1] We can look at this in the context of the famous definition of insanity: "Doing the same thing over and over again and expecting different results." I would expand on these definitions by saying wishful thinking is hoping that a situation or person will get better or change, even when (a) there is no evidence to support that hope, (b) no one is doing anything differently to bring about a change, and (c) no matter what is being promised, discussed, or proposed, history supports the conclusion that nothing will change.

Now I am not saying that hope is a bad thing. Quite the contrary, hope, like faith, is crucial. As Elie Wiesel said, "Just as man cannot live without dreams, he cannot live without hope."[2] But when it comes to being radically honest, to getting naked, we need to recognize the distinction between healthy hope, which is grounded in a realistic view of a situation, versus unhealthy hope, which is predicated upon wishful thinking or a desire for change without any evidence to support it. Thinking that you will finally get the promotion when you have been passed over three times, believing that your loved one will quit drinking on Monday when they make the same promise every Saturday, or trusting a friend with a confidence when they have betrayed you in the past are examples of wishful thinking. They're the kind of stories I hear from my clients. They are illusions, deceptions, things that we lie to ourselves about, falsehoods that keep us from being present to what is.

Take Laura, for example. She was a successful event planner. She lived her life as she planned her events—everything tied with a perfect bow, accented with tasteful and cheery touches, and accompanied by fun and fabulous party favors. She prided herself on being a kind and happy person. She felt like she had been given so many blessings in life, and from the outside looking in, she had it all.

She contacted me when she found herself in a pattern of denial. She *knew* something was off, and in fact, she had been very brave about confronting people in her life when her I AM was signaling something was wrong. But they kept telling her she was crazy. Wanting desperately to believe, Laura bought into their denial. By the time she met me, she had spent ten years hoping things would change on their own. Wishful thinking at its worst!

Laura had met Philip when she was in college and he was in law school. Although she had always wanted to be an attorney as well, after three years of dating, her dream of marriage and family was more compelling than a law degree. Philip was in no hurry to head to the altar, but after years of stalling he finally acquiesced, and Laura got her fairy-tale wedding. When they began their life together, things looked good. Philip's law practice was successful. They had a beautiful home, luxury cars in the driveway, and three beautiful children. Well liked in the community, Laura launched her event planning business. She dedicated her life to making her family and clients happy, but despite appearances, she never truly felt that way. She knew something was missing in her marriage—something was off with Philip, who often stayed out late and always seemed distant.

As years went by, she tried to approach Philip about his erratic and aloof behavior. Every time she brought it up, he explained it away by saying he was working late or entertaining clients. Even worse, he told her that she was crazy, making up stories and problems in her mind.

Laura tried to deny her unhappiness. She planned parties, social events, and trips and kept busy being the best mom possible. Still, her concerns about her husband lingered.

Soon Laura began to suspect that Philip had a drug problem. She even reached out to his mom for support when she found some drug paraphernalia in his car. As the old saying goes, "Like mother, like son." Philip's mother berated Laura for spying on Philip and told her to shut her mouth since she had a nice lifestyle. Laura did just that: she shut her mouth, swallowed her truth, and plastered a smile on her face.

Things remained status quo until one day when their oldest child went on a school trip and brought back rolls of film to be developed. Rushing to take them to the drugstore, Laura grabbed all the rolls of film she found in the kitchen. A few days later when Laura went to pick up the pictures, she was shocked at what she found. Two packets of photos were of Philip and a man Laura had never seen before. When she confronted her husband and asked him if he was having a relationship with a man, he once again told her that she was crazy and that they were just good friends goofing around.

At this point, Laura knew they needed help and convinced Philip to go to therapy with her. Unfortunately, Laura found no support for her feelings as the therapist sided with Philip, who portrayed Laura as the problem. She told Laura that she would be foolish to give up such a wonderful husband and lifestyle, and if she wanted to save her marriage for her children's sake, then she needed to be the one to make it work!

This is when Laura called me.

By safely and anonymously being coached over the phone, Laura gradually revealed the lie she was living and the feelings she was trying to avoid. I acknowledged the many times that she had listened to her I AM and the courage it took to confront Philip and his mom and to take her problems to the therapist. We talked about how sometimes living a life of integrity can be challenging and how, in the short-term, it often feels easier to settle and live in the illusion of wishful thinking. But ultimately the pain of ignoring your truth becomes too great. It was time for Laura to take her power back.

At this point, it was no longer even about what Philip said or did. It was about what was best for Laura. She was wasting away on her diet of wishful thinking, believing that her life was enough for her. She still felt that she "needed to know" exactly what Philip was doing before she could officially make the decision to leave.

To support her as she strengthened her muscle of self-trust, I invited her to go inside and tune in to her Integrity Alignment Monitor. I asked her to share what it told her.

I could hear the tears as Laura gasped for breath. Then she spoke up. "I think that Philip is involved with the man in those photographs. I think he has an entire secret life that I know nothing about."

Understanding how difficult it is to give up our wishful thinking, how easy it is to be sucked into other people's denial, and our need to see the truth in black and white, I supported Laura in coming up with an action plan that would help her find the truth.

Soon after our session, Laura decided to follow Philip. She ended up at a house in a different part of town. He went inside, and after a few hours, exited the house with the man from the pictures. Still trying to hold on to her last ounce of hope, Laura told herself that she still didn't have any actual proof about what went on behind closed doors. She wrote down the address of the house, called a private investigator, and asked him to research it.

A few days later, the investigator called back with shocking news. The house was in Philip's name! He and his lover had been sharing it for years.

With the truth in front of her, Laura called me in tears. In so many ways, she was angry at herself for how long she had allowed this to go on. She had inklings from early in their marriage, and yet she allowed herself to live in denial. It was easier than pushing back. But she was done living a lie. She divorced Philip and now feels lighter, stronger, and infinitely more self-assured because she is living her truth and honoring her intuition. Her new favorite phrase is "Don't mistake my kindness for stupidity!"

Wishful thinking is grounded in denial. It defines insanity. Because it is difficult to see that which is hidden, it's time to start looking!

⚡ **INTEGRITY INSIGHT**

- Where are you trapped in a cycle of wishful thinking?
- If you remove your blinders of wishful thinking, what will become clear to you as you access the truth?
- If you need a little help, ask yourself, "What would be immediately clear to someone else, if they looked at my situation?"

DENIAL INDULGER 2   **The Fairy Tale**

The fairy tale, or "someday" fantasy, is a close cousin to wishful thinking. Perpetuated by every story that ends with "and then they lived happily ever after," the someday fantasy has been ingrained into our psyches since childhood.

Although rooted in the same foundational fantasy as wishful thinking, our fairy tales tell us to wait, to hold on, because someday something magical will happen to lead us to our happily ever after. Fairy tales allow us to justify why we are not doing something in the present—we are waiting for something to happen. Someday fantasies are the "when . . . then" statements we all tell ourselves, such as these:

- When I lose twenty pounds, then I'll start going out and creating a social life.

- When my life calms down, then I will write my book.

- When I meet my soulmate, then I will travel.

- When my children go away to college, then I will live my life.

- When my parents pass, then I will come out of the closet.

- When I win the lottery, then I will pursue a career that I am passionate about.

Unlike wishful thinking, fairy tales may or may not be rooted in reality. The event that we are waiting for may or may not happen. But like all denial indulgers, they are vehicles out of the present moment and lies about why we are not living our life *now!* They cost us the experiences and feelings that we desire most because we put them off until a later day—a day that may or may not happen.

To wake up our inner Sleeping Beauty from the trance of the fairy tale, I like to ask, "Well, what if?" What if the soulmate never appears, you don't win the lottery, your parents continue to be healthy and thrive, your life never calms down? Then how are you going to still have a fabulous life?

When we step out of the fairy tale and start living in the now, we begin to see what is needed to make radical changes in our life *in the present,* to stop living in denial and realize a life of integrity. Don't wait until the end of your life to realize you had the power all along. *Your happily ever after can start today.*

⚡ INTEGRITY INSIGHT

- Start uncovering your "when . . . then" statements.
- Write down at least five.
- Ask yourself, "If the 'when' (the relationship, house on the beach, lottery win) never happens, then what are you going to do to still have a fabulous life?"

DENIAL INDULGER 3 Creatures of Habit

Most of us spend our days doing the same thing we did yesterday. We follow routines, stay consistent in our behaviors, and remain in our comfort zones. We become creatures of habit rather than conscious creators. Creatures of habit move through life on automatic pilot. Unlike those who are caught up in wishful thinking or asleep in the fairy tale, creatures of habit can be quite high functioning. Their denial comes in the form of their ability to live on automatic pilot. They are so busy doing what they have always done that they are no longer present to what they are doing, their motivations, whether their actions serve their highest purpose, or how they impact their I AM.

Creatures of habit stay in a job or relationship because it is familiar, push the boulder up the hill because they are the strong ones, continue to suffer and scrape along because they were taught that "life is about struggle." They meet their quotas and live inside the confines of the persona people expect them to be or the stereotypes that society has deemed acceptable. Although it is counterintuitive and comes at a cost, creatures of habit often accept the unacceptable because they are used to that way of being.

Judy was a powerhouse: smart, creative, beautiful, and charismatic. Although she had an entrepreneurial spirit and owned her own business, she was also a self-proclaimed "dream employee" since she was detail-oriented, worked hard, always showed up, and over-delivered.

Judy grew up in New York City. Her mother was a lawyer, her father an investment banker. From a material viewpoint, Judy had a privileged life, yet in their Park Avenue apartment, her parents fought constantly. Judy's father traveled a lot, and when he was away, her mother would take her anger and frustration out on Judy. She was both physically and verbally abusive.

Unconsciously committed to the someday fantasy that *When I am better, then Mom will be happy,* Judy became the "perfect" daughter. Although she excelled at all she did, Judy rarely received praise or any expression of love or affection from her mother. Judy became a creature of habit when it came to taking responsibility for others and ran as fast as she could on her treadmill of life, trying harder and harder, thinking it was her responsibility to make her mother happy.

Judy's father died when she was in her twenties. Shortly after, she met Brian. Fun, supportive, affectionate, attentive, and upbeat, Brian seemed to be all the things that her parents were not. He always saw the glass half full—a characteristic Judy had never encountered and that she fell in love with. Their relationship seemed magical, and they married within a year. Yet before long, everything changed. Brian's business declined, and he became physically, verbally, and emotionally abusive. He blamed Judy for everything that went wrong. Of course, Judy started to dance as fast as she could to make things better—once again thinking, *When I am better, things will get better.* To help alleviate some of the financial pressure the family faced, Judy launched a new business with a friend.

By the time I met Judy, she was exhausted and on the verge of a breakdown. Not only had she recreated her parents' marriage—a relationship filled with arguments and tension—she had reprised her role as the fixer, doer, and punching bag, once again committed to staying in the ring, but this time her justification was "for the sake of the children."

Judy and I began to examine her relationship with abuse. It was not her marriage to Brian, but a business deal that finally shut off her automatic pilot. A group of men who had invested in her business made a move to take it over. They tried to get rid of Judy and her partner, but when they realized how valuable Judy was to the company, they met with her privately to talk her into staying. Although they promised bonuses and opportunities, Judy knew something was off since they still wanted to cut out her partner. It was clear that they were not men of integrity, and one day they would do to her what they wanted to do to her partner.

As Judy told me what was going on, it became clear that these men were the next chapter in Judy's saga of enduring abuse. She realized that her capacity for abuse was vast. She saw that she had become so used to being the "strong one," while others loaded her up with more and more abuse, that she had lost sight of the difference between acceptable and unacceptable behavior!

It was time for Judy to step into her truth! She needed to recognize the persona she had created of always being able to handle everything for everyone and what it had cost her. She needed to wake up from her trance of denial and stop being a creature of habit. Through self-examination, Judy realized that the abused always becomes the abuser and that staying in abusive relationships and situations and putting the needs of others before her own was probably the most abusive act of all. Judy was able to walk away from her marriage and her business and allow herself the love, protection, and attention she had been longing for from others.

Being a creature of habit can be a powerfully destructive form of denial. Although many habits can be beneficial, if they enable us to step over our truth, it is time to strip down and look in that mirror.

⚡ INTEGRITY INSIGHT

In what ways do you live on automatic pilot? Do you mindlessly snack in front of the TV? Say yes when you mean no? Are you always running late? Consider the following questions:

- What are some of the habits or behaviors you automatically engage in? Make a list.
- What are the benefits of each of these?
- What are the costs of each of these?

DENIAL INDULGER 4
Our Perfectly Packaged Personas

Judy wrapped herself up in her persona of perfectionism. She, very much like me, was the overachiever, the strong and capable one, the fixer. Whether we realize it or not, we all have our established personas. The face we show the world often comes with routines and thoughts. Think of the eternal optimist who always has a big smile, wears cheery clothing, and constantly affirms that everything and everyone is "fantastic!" Or the person with the victim persona whose head is always down, looks a bit messy and disheveled, and exudes *Poor me! Why me?*

Like all denial indulgers, personas are protective mechanisms for the ego. They are generally born from shame or pain, or as the result of our shadow. We get so tightly wrapped in the persona we create that we cannot see how we appear to others. Not only can't we get naked, but we don't realize we are wearing a facade because it becomes affixed like a second skin. Some people, like my client Regina, spend a lifetime trying on personas, hoping that someday they will finally love the skin that they are in.

Regina grew up feeling invisible. There were so many children in her family that she believed her parents hardly noticed when she left their midwestern town after high school and moved to California to pursue a career in film. She got a job as a weather girl on a local news channel. Liking the feeling of being noticed and never wanting to be a "doormat" like her mother who stayed home and took care of everyone else but not herself, Regina continued to do whatever she could to be visible as she built her career. This included lots of men, drugs, and partying. Barely over twenty, Regina got pregnant. Although she wasn't 100 percent sure who the father was, she convinced herself that it had to be John, the most successful and powerful of the men she was with. John, who was older, liked having a beautiful younger woman on his arm. He agreed to marry Regina. Although she embraced her role as John's wife, she never truly felt that she fit in. She'd been raised to believe there were "haves" and "have nots" and that she was a "have not." So although she learned how to play the part of a successful man's wife, Regina always felt inadequate. Her belief became a reality when Regina found John in bed with another woman.

Feeling lost and not sure who she was, Regina decided to reinvent herself. She moved across the country, traded in her designer bag for a briefcase, and got a job as an office manager in a small law firm. Within a year, Regina found a new husband, and they created a nice, simple life. Before long, Regina got tired of her nice, simple life and decided she wanted more. This time the divorce was much more amicable, and once again Regina was on the move.

Knowing that something needed to shift, Regina began transformational work. She studied with many teachers, learned valuable concepts and healing modalities, and by the time I met Regina, she was a self-proclaimed "light being." She even dressed the part, with mala beads wrapped around her wrist, crystals on her neck, and T-shirts that proclaimed, "Choose Joy!" Totally sincere in her desire to support and inspire others, she wanted to work with me and eventually become a coach. However, when I worked with Regina, it became clear that she could not look at anything negative. She claimed to have "let go" of her past. Every statement that came out of her mouth was an affirmation. She was constantly saying things like, "The Universe will provide," and "What you can conceive and believe, you can achieve." She had a network of healers, psychics, and intuits that she consulted to support her decisions. She carried a pendulum, asked it questions, and let the swing of the pendulum dictate her choices.

Although I agree with the fundamental principles of most affirmations and the power of positive thinking, and I am open to seeing the value in a gifted person's insights, Regina had become overly dependent on her spiritual practices, and in doing so, became disempowered. Instead of looking inside herself and standing strong in her own integrity, she was constantly deferring to others.

A few weeks into our work together, Regina began to see how her fear of not being visible, of not mattering to the people in her life, had made her invisible to herself. She realized that she persisted in creating personas because she wanted to create a sense of belonging. She tried it with men, and when that didn't work, she looked to something greater, the Universe. Although it was a step in the right direction, she gave her power away to spiritual concepts and gurus. In believing that she had arrived by stepping into the persona of a "light being," she had lost her impetus for true growth.

Coaching became Regina's catalyst to make a U-turn back to herself. Learning to use and trust her own I AM, she tapped into the most powerful divination tool there is—the wisdom within her. Regina now looks to herself as her "guru" and loves the skin she is in.

Each of our personas blinds us from the truth and limits our self-perception, but the spiritual persona like the one Regina adopted is tricky. She couldn't see that in the name of empowerment she had given up her power—she was blinded by the light.

Personas keep us in denial. When we assume a persona, we are cut off from the totality of ourselves. It's time to wake up, stop being a caricature, and start connecting to the wisdom of who you *really* are.

⚡ INTEGRITY INSIGHT

Take a walk through your "closet"

- What personas have you been wearing?
- What is the image you have been trying to perpetuate in the world?

Don't make whatever you discover bad or wrong. Instead, see how it has served and limited you, and then begin to imagine what your expression of self would be if you loved the skin you're in.

DENIAL INDULGER 5   **Our Toy Box**

In May 2015, *Time* magazine reported on a study by the Microsoft Corporation that revealed the average attention span of humans had decreased from twelve to eight seconds—which is the same as that of a goldfish.[3] The decrease was attributed to the effects of our increasingly digitalized lifestyle.

Without question, we live in a world of distractions. In any moment, we can watch TV, surf the Internet on our laptop, text on our tablet, and talk on our smartphone. We spend hours every day, head down, checking our email, voicemail, texts, and social media.

We have built a world that supports indulging our denial. Although we think we are engaged and connected, our touchscreens make us *lose* touch! By staying plugged in, we have learned to tune out. By defining ourselves by our ability to multitask, we have lost our ability to commit. Through our illusion of connection, we have become not only disconnected from others, but from ourselves.

When I lead The Shadow Process, one of the guidelines for success is that people remain in silence when they are not in the actual workshop. During the first break, we invite them to call their families and let them know that unless there is an emergency, they won't be hearing from them for the next two and a half days. We suggest participants disconnect from TV, their phones, and computers when they go back to their hotel rooms. We encourage them to look at all the ways they detach from themselves, their feelings, and even their dreams and visions throughout their daily lives. We ask, "Can you imagine what would happen if you used the time you spent on social media to work on reaching your goals?"

Although beneficial, technology and social media can be life robbers and denial indulgers. It is our fear—fear of not wanting to feel something, fear of not wanting to face some truth, fear of not wanting to be with ourselves—that has us stay busy. Although we have all heard the saying, "He who dies with the most toys wins!" if you want to enjoy your life and those toys to the fullest, you need to turn off your distractions and sit with your discomfort. *The only way to break through your fear is to go through your fear.*

Social media, touchscreens, and mobile devices are not the only items in our toy boxes—they just happen to be the most prevalent. From overexercising and overentertaining to diet or sports obsessions—anything can become a distraction that keeps us unconscious, preoccupied, and out of integrity.

During my marriage, we built and lived a big life. We had three amazing children, an active social life, and demanding careers. I avoided dealing with my personal integrity issues by focusing on the next thing—the next birthday, vacation, party, sporting event. I don't know if the marriage got worse because of all the distractions, but I do believe the distractions kept a dying marriage alive. They kept us busy and enabled us to deny the elephant in the room.

⚡ INTEGRITY INSIGHT

What's in your toy box?

- What are your go-to distractions?
- What do they help you avoid?
- What issues, situations, feelings, or truths are obscured when you are preoccupied with a toy from your toy box?

Take It Off!

I hope you see by now that there is no more time for avoidance and denial. *We can't live in integrity if we are lying to ourselves.* So no, getting naked is not about stripping off your clothes. It's about getting quiet, connecting inside, and being radically honest about where you are at in the various areas of your life that are and are not working.

It's been said that *intimacy* means "into me I see!" If you want to be intimate with others, start by being intimate with yourself. Getting naked is about exactly that. It's about turning inward and facing the truth instead of running away. There's no more time for avoidance. The first step of the Integrity Process opens you up to look at your life with fresh eyes.

As you survey your personal landscape, avoid using what you discover in any area or situation to beat yourself up because that could discourage you. Instead, look through the eyes of fascination and the perspective of promise as you acknowledge what is and is not working.

Remember, integrity is not about perfection. There are no rewards for saying you're okay, pointing to your perfectly polished persona, and defending your assertion of how fine your life is. The rewards come from busting through wishful thinking, fairy tales, polished personas, busyness, and deceptions and living your deepest truths and grandest desires. The rewards come from self-liberation.

The Process

There's a reason this part of the book is called "The Integrity Process." It's because *personal transformation is a process.* Sometimes transformation happens in a moment, but to live a life of integrity, you must experience transformation moment by moment and be committed to looking deeper, uncovering the stories and beliefs that you repeat in your mind, understanding the influence they have on your choices, and acknowledging the current state of being that they have created. As you commit to this transformational process, remember that the deeper you dig, the more gold you will find. The question to ask yourself is not, *Am I out of integrity?* but *Where and how am I out of integrity?*

INTEGRITY IGNITER *It's Weigh-In Time!*

The Integrity Advantage is a total life makeover that invites you
to survey your life's landscape with a fresh perspective. Start
by honestly looking at where you *are* versus where you *want to
be*. You can begin with the areas I have listed in the worksheet
that follows, but feel free to add others that are relevant and
need addressing. Use the following guidelines to complete your
worksheet (and remember that you can download and print these
worksheets at soundstrue.com/integrity-advantage/worksheets):

Where I AM   On a scale of 1 to 10, with 1 being "not at all" and 10
being "totally," rate your level of satisfaction in each area of your life.

How I AM   On a scale of 1 to 10, with 1 being "none" and 10 being
"maximum," rate the effort you put into each area of your life.

How I AM Feeling   What are the feelings that are present as you
reflect on each of these different aspects of your life?

What I AM Experiencing   Acknowledge and describe what you are
experiencing at the present in these various aspects of your life.

Once you have completed your worksheet, consider the following:
- Are there any other areas or situations that feel out of whack
  or need some attention? If so, add them to your worksheet.
- Since we all have blind spots, try asking a trusted friend to
  share what they see in those areas that you can't. This can be
  tricky, though, since most people are not trained to be straight
  with another person and are looking at life through their own
  filters. So you can also try to trick your ego—pretend to be
  your own best friend and look at your life with compassionate
  yet analytical eyes.

GET NAKED WORKSHEET

	Where I AM	How I AM	How I AM Feeling	What I AM Experiencing
Health, Wellness, and Body				
Home, Surroundings, and Physical Environments				
Finances				
Career				
Friends				
Family				
Community and Connections				
Intimate Relationship				
Personal/ Spiritual Growth and Learning				
Fun, Leisure, and Enjoyment				
Service and Charitable Endeavors				
Life Balance and Flow				

7

STEP TWO   Busting Your Own BS

Every year I meet hundreds of people who seem to be working hard to reach their next level of success. They are caught up in *trying*—trying to diet, trying to go to sleep earlier, trying to take better care of themselves, trying to be financially responsible. But they are stuck in the trying phase; they are unable to break through to success.

Frustrated and ashamed of their inability to achieve their goals, they are quick to offer up an excuse—some justification, rationalization, or explanation for why they have not or cannot move powerfully forward. But just as it is said that "trying is lying," every time we are proffering an excuse, we are arguing for our limitations and sealing in a fate of failure. As Debbie Ford so eloquently said:

> Our excuses are automatic; they take no thinking or
> creativity. We all have them, we all use them, and we all
> pretend that we are rendered powerless by them. Some
> of our excuses are obvious and some are so subtle that
> it takes a very keen eye to expose them. Excuses are the
> proverbial back door that we leave open in case the pursuit
> of our goals is harder than we anticipated and we want to
> take a time-out. They are literally our attempt to "excuse"
> ourselves from fulfilling our objectives and behaving like
> the responsible, powerful, creative human beings that we
> are. Excuses transfer all of our inner power over to outer
> circumstances and strip away our ability to create results.[1]

Like a little child with dirty hands who claims they weren't playing in the mud, the exercise fanatic who is limping yet insists that everything is fine, the executive who falls asleep in meetings yet refuses to take a break, or the person who sits by the phone waiting for it to ring but defends an inattentive caller, saying, "They must be busy right now," at some point we all need to get real.

We need to recognize that underneath all the *trying*, excuses, justifications, rationalizations, and self-sabotaging behaviors lie an army of limiting beliefs, fears, laziness, self-doubt, and insecurities that undermine our resolve and keep us stuck and out of integrity. Although these disempowering thoughts are generally dressed up as long-winded, seemingly sound explanations, they are BS! Total BS.

And we've all got some!

No one likes change or dealing with things they want to avoid. We procrastinate. You say you'll start the diet on Monday. You'll make a budget after Christmas. You'll quit smoking or you'll stop eating standing up once things calm down at work. We have a neat pile of excuses, justifications, and rationalizations for why we *don't* do things:

- What's the point?

- It's someone else's job.

- It's not that important.

- No one will ever know.

- I'm not ready.

- Things never work out for me.

- I don't have time.

- They will get upset with me.

- No one is going to tell me what to do.

We have our justifications and rationalizations for why we *do* things that we know aren't best for us:

- I have no choice.

- I should do it for them.

- They will be disappointed if I don't.

- I need the money.

- I deserve to have one vice.

- They need me to.

- It's only this once.

- Just one more time.

- It doesn't count.

- Because I can.

And then, of course, we have our negative thoughts and limiting beliefs, those pesky integrity snatchers that keep us paralyzed:

- I am not good enough.

- I am not worthy of it.

- No one cares what I think.

- I am too old/young/fat/jaded/sensitive/
irresponsible/undisciplined.

- I don't matter.

- I don't know.

- I will be disappointed.

- I don't belong.

Our BS becomes so familiar and entrenched that we don't even see it for what it is: an excuse, a rationalization, a lie. We perceive our BS as facts. And we go so far as to provide evidence to support these so-called facts. Whenever someone says, "I can't," or "I am too busy," they always add the list of things they are doing or must do—evidence to justify what they see as not having time. But it's not fact—it's BS.

Why do we lie to ourselves? What are we so afraid of? Underneath our excuses and the bravado of our BS is an unwanted situation or emotion we are avoiding.

I'll give you an example from my own life.

I'm a Julia Roberts fan, and I always think of her movie *Runaway Bride* as the catalyst that helped me uncover some of my own BS. *Runaway Bride* is a romantic comedy about a perennial bride-to-be whose weddings become a string of misses as she continues to bolt every time she is about to walk down the aisle. After my divorce, I believed I would be married again within a year. I posted pictures of brides, diamond rings, and couples holding hands as they walked along the beach on my vision board. I was candid about wanting to get married or be in a committed relationship. Yet it wasn't happening. I had a series of relationships that each lasted about six months.

I knew that no matter what I said or thought, there had to be something else going on. I had to look at my own BS and what was causing me to be out of integrity. When I examined the situation, I realized that I was dating men who were nice guys but were not, as my friend Elaine would say, "my guy!" I saw that I was in a constant push-pull pattern with these men. When I got nervous about love and commitment (which was my I AM telling me something was off), I would start looking for what was wrong to justify pushing them away. But then my fear of being alone would take over. My voice of fear became so loud and paralyzing that it drowned out the whispers of my I AM, and before I knew it, when the guys had had enough and were heading for the door, I would reel them back in. That was my strategy. I also had my list of justifiable excuses as to why I couldn't commit: I was a single mother with three teenage girls, and I worked at night leading workshops and teaching. My BS was so good that I not only fooled others, but also myself. I was being a good mother and spending my time helping people, but I was never going to manifest the right relationship while I was caught up in a cycle of self-sabotage. It wasn't until I took the time to bust that BS that I could finally get clear about what was going on.

Whenever there is an area of our life where we are not creating what we say we want but feel like we are *trying, trying, trying*, there is an integrity issue. Whether we are conscious of it or not, our fear and beliefs are running our life. For me, it was limiting beliefs like *Love is not safe. You can't trust love. I can't have what I truly desire. On some level, I am not special enough to be loved.* These fears and beliefs came from unhealed wounds in my past that were influencing my adult life when it came to relationships.

Most of our wounding, or the formation of our limiting belief system, happens when we are young, under the age of ten. This wounding is generally not accessible by our conscious minds. We often don't even remember the events that caused the wounding. They fade into our unconscious as do the limiting thoughts and beliefs we assigned to those events. But out of sight does not mean out of mind.

Anytime we are controlled by our wounded ego, we revert to the time of the original wounding, and our little-child self runs our show. When I begin to feel afraid, find myself blaming others, pushing them away, or isolating and trying to keep myself "safe," I always picture myself as a little girl with pigtails running upstairs to shut herself in her room so that she would not get in trouble. Although our little-child self is doing the best it can to keep us safe, it does not have the life experience or mental wherewithal to make high-level decisions.

Anytime our adult body is being run by our little-child self or wounded ego, we are working at limited capacity.

Day after day, I hear stories of people who have unconsciously developed strategies that help them avoid uncomfortable situations. They are the ones who:

- Always break up with their partner, so
  they don't ever get broken up with

- Have so many things on their to-do list that
  they always have a reason why they haven't
  tackled the big task or the one they fear

- Are people pleasers and spend all their time
  doing for others instead of themselves

- Remain in a state of overwhelm or confusion,
  so they can't commit to one thing

- Stay busy at work, so they don't have to
  deal with their issues at home

Although the psyche is brilliant, the wounded ego, when it is running our day-to-day life, is not. Our wounded ego creates excuses and strategies to avoid our truth. Kent is a great example of how our BS can completely run, rule, and ruin our life. His wife, Kristina, attended The Shadow Process Workshop and was so inspired by the insights she received that she encouraged Kent to attend. Kent said very little in his workshop, but I could tell he was engaged in everything that was being shared and all the exercises. I ran into Kent at the airport after the workshop, and he spoke to me about his life. He explained that he and his wife had been having issues in their marriage and that they both were committed to working on their relationship. It was evident that Kent loved his wife and was eager to do his work and look at how he was co-creating some of their problems. A short time after I returned home, I started working with Kent one-on-one.

Kent had grown up in a relatively small town in Europe with his younger brother, mom, and dad. His father, a schoolteacher, was injured in a car accident that left him with a hip injury and unable to engage in athletic activities. It also left him in pain, which he dulled by drinking. Kent's father tended to go out after work and come home stumbling drunk. When Kent's father was in the house, everybody had to be quiet since he needed to nap. The household atmosphere was incredibly tense. It was filled with either constant fighting between Kent's parents or a deathly silence when Kent's father was napping. Both of Kent's parents were critical, and as the eldest son, Kent received most of the blame and judgment. Eventually, Kent's father began to beat him. If he dared to cry, he was called weak and was shamed.

A good little boy who wanted only for his parents to stop fighting and to be loved, Kent internalized his parents' rejection and the verbal and physical violence. He took it to mean that he was unlovable and not good enough—he was the problem. As a little boy, Kent spent hours hiding behind the couch—afraid to be seen, speak, or even breathe. The strategy he learned to protect himself was to make himself invisible; not to share, communicate, or show any feelings; and most of all, to avoid conflict at any cost.

After enduring the drama of his parents' marriage, Kent swore he would never get married, but the minute he met Kristina, he changed his mind. Kristina had a big personality, and in their relationship, they played hard and fought hard. Despite the tumultuous dynamic they developed, they got married. Kent said that during fifteen years of marriage, there had been more ups and downs than he could count. Being run by the belief that he was "not good enough" and schooled since childhood to blame any and every problem on himself, Kent believed he was the cause of most of the issues in his marriage.

As we began to work together, I tried to help Kent identify some of his excuses that perpetuated this cycle of "not good enough" in his marriage. Kent justified not changing by telling himself things like *It's not that bad. This is normal. Everyone goes through it. It will get better.*

We soon identified these as excuses, and the excuses as BS. If he continued to live from this state of "lack consciousness," nothing would change, except that one day his wife would leave!

He also began to identify the strategies he used to avoid the feelings and ramifications he experienced as a scared little boy. He believed that if he spoke up about how he felt, things would get worse. Because of this, he:

- Never shared his feelings

- Never told his wife no or what he truly wanted

- Lied and told half-truths in order not to upset his wife

- Pretended things were fine

- Isolated himself

The interesting thing was that when I asked Kent if he guarded his words and thoughts at work, he replied, "Absolutely not! I am very outspoken and opinionated at work." Realizing how well respected he was in the workplace, and the impact of being self-expressed in that area of his life, I suggested that he start acting and being the same way at home.

A few months into our coaching relationship, Kent and Kristina were in the process of moving to a new house. One night, they were out at dinner, and although they were having a pleasant time, by the end, Kristina told Kent that she was not sure they should move together and that maybe it was time for them to separate. Kent listened to Kristina. The waiter came with the bill. They paid and walked out of the restaurant. Kristina took his hand on the way home. Telling himself that her gesture meant everything was okay, Kent never responded to Kristina's statements. They went home, went to sleep, and the next morning when Kristina came down for coffee she was furious. How could he say nothing when she brought up separating? She accused Kent of once again being inconsiderate, a coward, and making her feel invisible and unimportant.

It was in that moment that Kent realized that his BS was truly ruining his life. Yes, Kristina was a force to be reckoned with, but it was time for the little boy to come out from behind the couch and start acting like he did at work—as the man sitting at the desk. Since then, Kent has been bringing love and compassion to his wounded child. At home, the boy has become the man. He and Kristina are communicating more authentically and openly. They moved to their new apartment together and are both committed to working on their relationship.

It's Time for a Treasure Hunt

Confronting your BS is one of the best things you will ever do for yourself. You cannot live in integrity if you are lying, right? You've got to clear the patterns of your past that keep you stuck, small, and scared. They keep you from having a life you love.

In fact, underneath all that BS, you might find something surprising.

I've heard that one of President Ronald Reagan's favorite stories, written by an unknown author, is entitled "There's a Pony in There Somewhere!" It goes like this:

> There were two five-year-old boys, identical twins, one of whom was a pessimist and the other an optimist. Wondering how two boys who were identical on the outside could be so different on the inside, their parents took them to a psychiatrist.
>
> The psychiatrist took the pessimist to a room piled high with new toys, expecting the boy to be thrilled. But instead, the boy burst into tears.
>
> Puzzled, the psychiatrist asked, "Don't you want to play with these toys?"
>
> "Yes," the little boy bawled, "but if I did, I'd only break them."
>
> Next the psychiatrist took the optimist to a room piled high with horse manure. The boy yelped with delight, clambered to the top of the pile, and joyfully

dug out scoop after scoop, tossing the manure into the
air with glee.

"What on earth are you doing?" the psychiatrist asked.

"Well," said the boy, beaming, "there's got to be a
pony in here somewhere!"

As you start digging around in your BS, realize that there's a pony in
there somewhere! Okay, maybe not a pony, but you will find deep
insights into patterns that have probably been there since childhood.

Don't use what you uncover to beat yourself up, or berate yourself.
We don't have control over what happened in the past. But we do have
control over what we make it mean and where we go from here.

INTEGRITY IGNITER *Bust Your Own BS!*

Ask yourself the following questions:

- In what situations in your life are you in a cycle of *trying*?
  *Trying to make a change, trying to make something
  better, trying to fix something—these are the areas
  where there is a discrepancy between what you say
  you want and what you are experiencing. These are
  integrity issues.*

- What are the excuses, justifications, and rationalizations
  that keep you stuck or in this state of trying?
  *What are the excuses, justifications, and rationalizations
  for why you do things you shouldn't, and why you don't
  do things you know you want to?*

**Now picture yourself as that scared little child and ask yourself
these questions:**

- What behaviors does that scared child tend to engage
  in? What do they do to keep themselves safe? Do they
  hide behind the couch, like Kent, avoiding any kind of
  conflict or confrontation? Or like Kelley, do they leave
  before they are left, or push away before they get hurt?

- How is that scared child still running your adult body? What are the emotions you are trying to avoid? What are the strategies you now use to circumvent unwanted emotions and circumstances?

Now dig deep—it's time to find the pony! Identify situations in your life where there is a discrepancy between what you say you want and what you are experiencing. These may be situations you identified above that you are in a cycle of *trying* to change, or perhaps others will come up. Trust whatever comes up.

Use a separate copy of the worksheet that follows for each of these situations and use the following guidelines to complete each one:

Reality   Describe the situation as it exists today. What is the reality of the situation in the present?

Desire   Describe your vision of this situation. What is your grandest desire?

How Long   How long has this situation been this way? How long have you been struggling or not manifesting what you desire?

Excuses   What are the excuses you use that keep the situation as is?

Limiting Beliefs   What are the limiting beliefs you hold that prevent you from doing anything differently?

Patterns/Behaviors   What are the patterns and behaviors you engage in that lead you further away from what you say you want instead of closer to it?

Bust Your BS   How are the excuses, limiting beliefs, patterns, and behaviors all just a cover-up for your BS? How is it all BS?

Cost   What is the cost of living inside your BS? How has it impacted the other aspects of your life? Others' lives? Your emotions?

Live BS-Free   If you were living BS-free, what could you think, say, and do differently to create a different result?

BUSTING YOUR OWN BS WORKSHEET

Situation	
Reality	
Desire	
How Long	
Excuses	
Limiting Beliefs	
Patterns/Behaviors	
Bust Your BS	
Cost	
Live BS-Free	

8

STEP THREE Shift Happens

Okay, friends, step three. You're two down. You've gotten naked and radically honest. You've taken a brutal look at the BS that has been running your life. Now you are ready for the next step—a critical one that we often miss. Just because you got naked and busted yourself of your own BS does not mean you accept your life as it is *right now*. A road often needs to be paved between acknowledgment and acceptance. Just because you can point and say, "Look at that," does not mean you accept that! To change something, we must first acknowledge what is and then accept it as it is.

Do you know how long I was married? Probably not because I haven't told you yet. Remember my story at the beginning of the book, where I talked about all the warning signs that were present on my wedding day? The ones I ignored in pursuit of what I thought made sense? You may have assumed, *Wow, that marriage couldn't have lasted five years! Who can go into a marriage knowing that the person isn't right and stay with them?*

Well, yeah, but that's why I'm writing this book. I was as entrenched in excuses, BS, and personas as anyone.

I was married for thirteen years.

Yep. I stepped over my truth for thirteen years. Obviously, there were many times when I acknowledged that things weren't working. But I was so scared to take that next step, to accept that the marriage had failed, that it would not change, that it was over and I needed to get out.

This going from acknowledgment to acceptance is the demarcation point where shift can happen.

Acceptance is being able to recognize and be with what is. It is a fundamental step in the journey to living in integrity. You cannot get to where you want to be without clearly knowing and truly owning where you are starting from *at this moment*: that is what acceptance is all about. It is not about judging or punishing yourself. It is about knowing yourself, embracing yourself, and knowing that change is possible.

My Personal Journey from Acknowledgment to Acceptance

I'm always amazed at what good actors we are. We learn these skills early in life—to have a tough exterior, to not reveal what is going on inside, to not let people see you sweat, and of course, to smile. We create facades and illusions of what our life "should be" and they can be exhausting to sustain or draining to keep chasing. My facade was the so-called perfect marriage with the so-called successful husband. We had a beautiful house, three beautiful daughters, and a busy social calendar. We "had it all."

Just as beauty needs to be more than skin deep to endure, the funny thing about facades is when you feel that the one you have carefully crafted is about to be torn off, it is easy to become desperate, to do whatever it takes to keep up pretenses and prevent the walls from tumbling down.

A few years before my marriage officially ended, my then husband moved out. During one of our many fights, my husband told me he needed to get away and was going to drive down to Key West for the weekend to think things through. A few days after he returned, we had another huge fight. The next day, he told me that he had rented an apartment and would be moving out.

Even though deep down I knew that this was where our marriage was headed, I was devastated and desperate to maintain the facade for a little longer. I still wasn't ready to take that towel off that I had been hiding under since my wedding day. Three kids later, I was even more deathly afraid to admit that our marriage wasn't working. I remained steadfast in my denial that separation would be best for everyone. I did more than stay in my denial. I did what any well-trained lawyer would do: I argued and fought to keep my denial firmly in place by trying to control the situation and manipulate the outcome by asking questions like, "What would we tell the children?" and "How would this impact their lives?" and "Couldn't we try another therapist?"

Ultimately, my strategies won out. My husband appeased me by saying that since he was traveling for business, he would come home one or two days during the week and then move to his apartment on the other days when he wasn't traveling. The arrangement would not appear much different on the outside, and our girls were too young to notice or question the truth. Desperate, I agreed to this arrangement. It allowed me to put a bandage on the facade that was crumbling down around me. *Little did I realize that this bandage was not helping me heal, but instead the adhesive kept the "dis-ease" firmly entrenched in my body and poisoning my self-esteem.*

I asked him to show me his apartment. I wanted to see where he was going to be staying when he wasn't at home. When we walked in the door, my heart dropped. It was all set up with dishes in the cabinets, sheets on the bed, and a working phone line. It was obvious that he had been planning this or even had the apartment for a while. Resentment raged as I seethed, "How dare you?" I should have been the one to tell him to get the hell out and stay the hell out. I should have been the one to call the shots, but instead he was the lead negotiator.

Deep down I knew why I was incapable of demanding the change we both knew was necessary. *I was more consumed by fear than I was by anger.* I did not think I could make it on my own. I had created a whole story, which was more like a nightmare, about what would happen to me and my children if I got divorced. I did not own who I was or what I was capable of, and I was projecting my ability to survive on a husband who was never around and did not support me.

Every weekend, as my husband got ready to leave for his apartment, I stood in our bathroom watching him pack, and I would break down crying. I didn't want him to go. Fear allowed me to think that a shoddy marriage was better than being on my own.

One Friday, a few weeks into this new arrangement, a miracle happened. I didn't break down on the day he left. I watched him pack, but there was no story swirling around in my head. I skipped the "please don't go" dramatics. I was beginning to reconnect with my self-worth and realize that I would be fine without him. I was starting to understand that I deserved more, was more, and could become more.

Ironically, that Monday when he came home, he told me that he was giving up the apartment. He was planning to move back in.

I remember thinking that he left too fast and came back too soon. Right there, I could have said no! I wanted to say, "No! I am okay on my own. I want you to move out for good." But instead, I choked down my truth, received him back in the house with a lackluster hug and a sharp pain in my heart, and settled for two more years of torture that robbed me of my integrity.

Enough Is Enough

Our last and most expensive psychiatrist said, "Your marriage will never change. You need to get a divorce." That's when I accepted I could no longer sustain false hope or live inside an illusion of wishful thinking.

Looking for more guidance, signs that this was finally it, I asked the Universe for confirmation by having a reading with a well-known astrologer. During the reading, which was recorded, I asked her questions about divorce, separation, and whether I had a second marriage in my chart. I left the tape of the session in my car and listened to it as I drove around totally consumed with thoughts about my marriage.

Summer arrived, the kids were away at camp, and I went to a weekend workshop in California. While I was away, something happened to my husband's car and he borrowed mine. When he started the car, the tape that was in the cassette player came on, and he heard my entire astrological session. When I got back from my trip, he told me what had happened, how he had heard my conversation with the astrologer, and asked me what I wanted to do. After a long discussion, we decided to stay together through October, when we would celebrate our two eldest daughters' B'not Mitzvah, a celebration in the Jewish religion when two or more girls twelve or older take on the responsibility of an adult. We agreed that after this major family milestone, we would separate.

The night of the B'Not Mitzvah was one of the lowest points of my life. The theme of the party was the Academy Awards, and there were three-foot Oscar statues made of chocolate and spray-painted in a gold dust on each table. Like most of the Bar and Bat Mitzvahs in our community at that time, it was an evening of opulence and excess. The champagne flowed, the food was abundant, and a twelve-piece band played all the hits. There we were, dressed up as the perfect family in our gold gowns, husband wearing a matching bow-tie. We were surrounded by two hundred family members and friends. Everybody, or almost everybody, was having a ball, except me. My husband and I had only perfunctory interaction. We hardly danced, spoke, or connected. The pain of the charade was so great that I couldn't wait for the evening to end and everyone to leave!

However, the situation that triggered and saddened me the most happened as we left the celebration. Since the party took place at one of the big hotels on South Beach, we booked a bunch of rooms to let our girls and their closest friends stay overnight. As we entered the elevator after the party ended, in popped one of my closest friends with her boyfriend. They were holding a bottle of champagne and two glasses. They were arm in arm, physically and emotionally connected, all smiles and going up to a room that they had booked to keep celebrating. I looked at them and wondered, *What is wrong with this picture? We are the couple that had what was supposed to be "the night of all nights," a major milestone in our family history, yet this other couple is the one with the champagne in hand and joy in their hearts.*

That was it for me! I could no longer exist inside a story of disconnection, deceit, and disgust. I could no longer live so far out of my integrity. I could no longer perpetuate the lie. But we still had one more party to attend the next weekend. It was a combination birthday and Halloween party for a close friend. I promised to keep the facade alive for one more week, but then it would be time.

Short on imagination and desire, we put together last-minute costumes and went to our friend's party. It didn't take long before my husband and I both adopted our party personas. He was doing his thing, and I was off to the side, trying to pretend it was okay but pissed off and embarrassed on the inside. In the past, dutiful wife that I tried to be, I used to smile or laugh to show that I thought he was funny, unfazed by his actions, and that I was aligned with his "humor," instead of the brunt of it. But this time, I had checked out. I could no longer laugh, remain stoic, fake it, or even stay at the party for another minute. I realized that once our marriage ended, I would no longer have to pretend the unacceptable was acceptable. I had had enough. I was not willing to live in denial or pretend for another minute. I decided to leave the party.

I had never walked away before. I had never truly declared, "Enough is enough," and that I was done. It felt damn good to take that step toward freedom!

That's what finally coming into alignment with your integrity does. It allows you to finally feel like the chains are off. *It is a declaration of liberation!*

The next day, my husband and I told people we were separating, and that was it. The road of the separation, divorce, selling the house, and moving was hard, but the day the judge signed our divorce papers, I went to court wearing a T-shirt under my jacket that said, "Freedom." I instructed my attorney that the moment the judge signed the divorce decree, he was to visualize me flying into my new life. As hard as the decision to get divorced had been, it had been harder to be out of integrity with myself.

> Two roads diverged in a wood, and I—
> I took the one less traveled by,
> and that has made all the difference.
>
> ROBERT FROST, "The Road Not Taken"

Forks in the Road

The bridge between acknowledgment and acceptance is often a place in the transformational process where people get stuck—and they can remain, like I did, in that place for years, or even forever. But there are demarcation points on every journey, forks in the road, where we can choose to rise above the level of consciousness we are operating on and take a higher road. We can keep doing things the way we always have and stay stuck. Or we can make the leap, accept what is wrong, and finally make the changes we need to make. We can fly to freedom.

Distinguishing between fact versus fiction, truth versus thoughts, experience versus expectation, right versus wrong, and faith versus fear are tools we can use when we reach those forks to aid us in making shifts happen.

FORK 1 Fact versus Fiction

As I discussed earlier, we each have hundreds of stories running through our heads at any given time. Our stories consist of the thoughts, beliefs, and interpretations we wrap around any event. We then see our future situations, experiences, and people through the lens of our stories that we've developed from the past. These stories include who we define ourselves to be, our relationships with other people, and our issues with things like money, our body, happiness: *I didn't get the promotion because I'm not smart enough. The opposite sex is not attracted to me because I'm not thin enough. I'll never have enough money.*

I love the quote by Anaïs Nin that says, "We don't see things as they are; we see them as we are."[1]

This is because of our meaning-making mechanisms—we wrap a meaning around every event. They can be positive meanings: *I'm getting a divorce because I deserve more.* Or they can be negative meanings: *I'm getting a divorce because I'm not good enough.* One of the reasons it took me so long to accept that my marriage was over was because of the negative connotations I had attached to what it would mean about me that I was a divorced woman, what it would mean for my children that they came from a broken home, and what my future would look like if I were alone.

But my fear about what it meant that I was divorced, what it meant that my kids came from a broken home, was just that, FEAR:

> False
> Evidence
> Appearing
> Real

It wasn't reality. I didn't know who I would become as a divorced woman. Instead, I had attached a bunch of lies to what that event would entail.

It was time to face the facts and stop believing the fiction. In my case, the fact was I was getting divorced. The fiction that I wrapped around that fact was as follows: *I failed. I was so stupid. I will die alone. I am ruining my children's lives.*

It was these fictions that caused me pain, sealed in my suffering, and kept me from the release of acceptance.

Look at what thoughts are running through your mind about the situations you face. Are you listening to facts or fiction? The journey to acceptance means facing the facts and throwing the fictions away. When you're at a fork in the road, focusing on facts over fiction will help you choose a different path.

FORK 2   Truth versus Thoughts

Distinguishing thoughts from the truth is the next tool that will aid us in making shifts happen.

I will never find a love like that again. I am different and will never belong. Life will disappoint me. There is no such thing as happiness. These are thoughts. They are interpretations of events, not grounded in truth. Your thoughts might seem like a momentary truth, but they are not truth. They are fictions.

One thought can be replaced by another thought. Anytime I start with "stinking thinking," I remind myself that I'm caught up in a thought and can always choose a new one. I visualize a shelf of thoughts and imagine pulling a different one off the shelf. Neither thought is more true than the next; they are all my fictions—so I have a choice. Do I want to hang on to a thought that imprisons me or replace it with one that empowers me? If we want to live a different story, we need to change the script. We need to shift from the negativity of the meaning-making machine saying, "I am not . . ." to the guidance of the Integrity Alignment Monitor, which will always support us in seeing that "I AM . . ."

Acceptance is about I AM.

⚡ INTEGRITY INSIGHT

Your meaning-making machine says, "I am not . . ."
while your Integrity Alignment Monitor says, "I AM . . ."
Try the following exercise:

- Observe how quickly your mind jumps into that meaning-making "I am not . . ." mind-set.
- When you identify a negative thought from your meaning-making machine, practice labeling it as that. See yourself deleting it, throwing it away, and picking a new empowering thought from the shelf—one that is infused with the power of I AM!
- Envision and feel yourself consciously coding that empowering thought into every cell of your body.

FORK 3 Experience versus Expectation

An *expectation* can be defined as the act or state of anticipating a certain outcome. Expectations are the "shoulds" and "should nots" that we put on ourselves, others, or the world. They are our attachments to how we think things should be. Anytime we are in a place of expectation or attachment, we are not in the experience of what is. Even worse, we are judging and critiquing the present, which puts us in a story of disappointment, betrayal, resignation, anger, and helplessness. Our expectation of how things should be keeps us from accepting what is. Ask Mindy.

When Mindy first contacted me, it was because she did not know what to do about her marriage. She had been married to Jack for twenty years and angry at him for as long. Mindy met Jack while they were both on a ski vacation. They lived on opposite sides of the country, so their courtship consisted of meeting in interesting places and taking fun trips. After a quick engagement, they got married, and Mindy acquiesced to move to Jack's hometown in the Carolinas for a year to see if she liked it. Mindy didn't, but Jack had no intention of moving. His family and business were both there. Mindy felt duped—in more ways than one. In her eyes, Jack became a different person after they got married. He was no longer fun, spontaneous, and free spirited. Instead, he was fearful, disconnected, and sarcastic. He had become his father, a cynical, unhappy man. She would have left him long before had it not been for the birth of their daughter, who was now fifteen, and her attachment to how a family should be. Mindy busied herself in her role as mother and escaped to their beach house when she needed to get away from Jack.

Shortly after Mindy and I started working together, I knew that this was about more than whether Mindy stayed in her marriage. For Mindy to have the life of her dreams, she had to look at the ways she was perpetuating her pain and giving up her power. She had to discover what in her past had caused her to handle situations the way she did. She needed to get to that place where shift happens!

Mindy had a tumultuous background. Her parents fought constantly until the day her father left. Her mother was critical, and her brother was mean spirited. Scared to be at home, from a young age Mindy spent as much time as she could at her friends' houses. She was always looking for her dream family.

This pattern followed Mindy throughout most of her dating life. She would become interested in a man, and if he came from a warm family, she would fall in love with his family. This didn't work out well for Mindy because the family was not always looking for a new daughter, and while the family was off living their own life, Mindy was left dating a man she had lukewarm feelings for. When she met Jack, she thought she had hit the jackpot. He was fun and exciting, and his mother immediately labeled her "the daughter she never had" and vowed that they would have "so much fun together." But that never happened. When Jack's mother showed up, she always had a gift in hand but never stayed long. Mindy wasn't just angry with Jack, but also with his mother. Neither had turned out to be what she expected!

Mindy realized that because of her upbringing she had unconsciously created core beliefs that were running her life: *No one is there for me. I am not enough. I can't trust anyone. What I want doesn't matter. I am not important.*

She came to see that it was her attachment to how Jack and his mother *should* act, and her continued expectation that they would respond differently, that was causing her so much angst. She blamed them for not caring about her or being there for her, and she used this as the excuse to keep running away from Jack and the situation, as she had done for almost twenty years.

Mindy started to see how her expectations that Jack and his mother should or would be different kept reopening her core wounds of feeling unimportant or that she did not matter. When we spoke about the gift of acceptance, Mindy started to distinguish between what she was experiencing and what she expected. If she measured her marriage and mother-in-law by what she expected, they would always fall short. But being able to look realistically at what she was experiencing opened her up to seeing a new perspective. The road of expectations always leads to pain. Being present to what she was experiencing led her to the possibility of a new path.

There was good in her life with Jack. They had a beautiful home and daughter, a great beach house she loved. She had lots of flexibility since she did not work, and Jack never complained if she traveled with friends or with their daughter. She even started to see Jack's mother in a different light—she was doing the best she could and was a good grandmother. Mindy learned to pay less attention to them and more attention to herself. Realizing that her unmet expectations put her in a place of resignation, she created a vision for what she wanted in her life, and she got back her *joie de vivre*. All this because she separated experience from expectation!

FORKS 4 AND 5   Right versus Wrong, Faith versus Fear

Debbie Ford's book *The Right Questions* is based on the premise that your life reflects the choices you make, and if you ask yourself the right questions, you are more apt to make better choices. She lists ten powerful questions that support you in making high-level choices. Two of the questions she poses in that book that can support you in finding acceptance are these:

- Am I looking for what's right or am I looking for what's wrong?

- Is this an act of faith or an act of fear?

Looking for what's wrong keeps us in our story of victimhood. It per-petuates that negative meaning-making machine. It keeps us fighting the present and out of integrity with trusting that we, and every-thing, are as they should be. As Debbie says, "If we look for what is wrong in any given situation, we will find it."[2] When we look for what is wrong, we cannot see what is right in front of us or that there is another road we were meant to take. It keeps us stuck fighting for the way we think it should be, even when everyone else has moved on. Looking for what is right shifts the lens of our experience. Look-ing for what's right fosters acceptance. It gently guides and nudges us along that road from acknowledgment to acceptance.

Our meaning-making machine is run by our voice of fear. To quiet the noise of our voice of fear and turn down the volume of our meaning-making machine, we need to counterbalance it with a calming and potent voice—the voice of faith. Bringing faith to our fear, we can stand in the knowing that whether we realize it or not in that moment, there is a divine design to life, and whatever is happening is happening for our soul's evolution. Taking the journey from fear to faith allows us to experience the freedom of acceptance.

Getting into Gear

When I walked into The Shadow Process Workshop for the first time, the first words I heard Debbie say were, "Transformation is a shift in perception." The Shadow Process is designed to support you in having shift after shift in perception—the way you view your life, others, your past, your present, and your future. Your life alters because of the state and level of consciousness you bring to every moment. Accep-tance happens when you shift your level of consciousness. When you drive your car in first gear, you can only go so fast—you need to shift gears to go faster. Similarly, shifting into the space of acceptance will allow you to move forward in a way you never thought possible. When you look at the same issue through a different lens, you will see it in a new light.

Shift happens!

And this shift in perception has the power to change what is possible.

INTEGRITY IGNITER *Time to Make Shift Happen!*

Start by becoming present to the distinction between **acknowledgment and acceptance.** What situations in your life are you still having a hard time accepting? These are the ones that you have created a story around about why they should not be as they are.

To help bridge the gap between acknowledgment and acceptance, take any situation (preferably the one you are having the hardest time accepting) and describe it in the worksheet that follows. Use the following guidelines to complete your worksheet:

I Am Not versus I AM What are the disempowering interpretations your meaning-making machine assigns to the situation versus the positive ones from your I AM?

Fictions versus Facts What are the stories you tell yourself about the situation versus the black-and-white facts?

Thoughts versus Truths What are the negative thoughts that automatically pop up about the situation versus other powerful truths you could replace these with?

Expectations versus Experiences What are the expectations you had for the situation—how did you hope it would turn out—versus what you are experiencing?

Wrong versus Right What do you see is wrong about the situation versus what you see that is right about it exactly as it is?

Fear versus Faith What does your voice of fear say about the situation versus what your voice of faith says?

SHIFT HAPPENS WORKSHEET

Situation_____

I Am Not	I AM
Fictions	Facts
Thoughts	Truths
Expectations	Experiences
Wrong	Right
Fear	Faith

Check back in. What can you now see about this situation? How can you see it as it should be? What do you now see that will support you in shifting from acknowledgment to acceptance?

What is an action step you could take this week to help you integrate this new perspective and move you forward on the road from acknowledgment to acceptance?

Use copies of this worksheet at any time to help you shift any and all future situations you have trouble accepting.

9

STEP FOUR   The Blessings
of Your Binges

There I was, racing around my kitchen, looking for the next thing to shove into my mouth. From cupboard to drawer, fridge to freezer, rummaging, searching for something—be it sweet or savory—to eat.

Wait a minute. I thought my days of self-sabotage were over!

I had to stop and ask: *What is going on? What am I trying to avoid? What truth am I trying to stuff down with food?*

This was not about physical hunger, but the emotional weight of something far greater.

The next step in the Integrity Process is to look at what I call our binges. Just like a dieter might ingest calories and foods that were not part of their plan, or a person trying to save money will blow their budget on an expensive pair of shoes, we all have times where we make less skillful choices for our life—choices that we know will lead to trouble. Those choices, like too many calories or credit card charges, have consequences.

The good news is that our self-sabotage reveals the keys to our freedom. It's time to examine when we binge, become fascinated, and discover the true impetus for those binges.

We all have our favorite forms of self-sabotage. For me, it was food. When there was an issue I didn't want to deal with, I ate. When there was an emotion I didn't want to feel, I ate. When there was a truth I didn't want to face, I ate. When I couldn't speak up or do it my way, I ate. I was an emotional eater, using food to fill my emotional needs or keep me from feeling any emotions at all. When I was on a binge, nothing could stop me. I was like a woman possessed. I would consume large amounts of food before I knew what I had done.

This behavior went on for decades. I tried everything I could to fix myself—to hide, change, or out-muscle my binge behavior. I tried every diet imaginable, therapy, and hypnosis. I put pictures of beautiful women on my bathroom mirror and refrigerator door and signs on the kitchen cabinets that read, "Stop, You Fat Pig!" I even wore a teeth-whitening apparatus, thinking that if I had the tray in my mouth, I wouldn't want to take it out and wipe off the yucky gel in order to eat. Yet where there is a will, there is a way, and none of my tricks worked. Nothing deterred me when it came to a good binge.

Like the person who wakes up with a hangover or with a one-night-stand in their bed, the aftereffects of a binge are never pleasant. Our internal choir of condemnation and criticism shouts, *What is wrong with you? How could you be such a loser? How could you possibly mess up again?*

My self-sabotage always led to a tirade of negative talk and self-judgment, which led to more shame and feelings of unworthiness. This resulted in one of two behaviors. Sometimes, it would send me straight back to the kitchen since the pain and shame of cheating on myself and being such a failure were so great that I had to numb them. Other times, it would lead me to the negotiating table with myself and the promises of how I would be better, what I would do differently, how things would change and my life would become perfect. Although I did not realize it at the time, my promises about how I would fix my life only reinforced my feelings of brokenness, damage, and not being good enough, which ultimately always led me right back to—that's right—the kitchen.

> Transformation does not happen when we fix it on
> the outside; it happens when we love it on the inside.

I spent years on the treadmill of self-sabotage and self-hatred until one day, as I was in the middle of one of my eating frenzies, I froze and checked in with myself: *What is going on with you?*

It must have been a moment of divine grace that allowed me to stop and realize the madness. In that moment, with that question, I took a deep breath and exhaled my pent-up, suppressed emotions. I stepped into what was happening within me instead of running away from it. I realized that my binges were signs from the Universe; they were a blessing because they were emerging to show me that something was off, that somewhere in my life there was an issue I didn't want to face, an emotion I didn't want to feel, a truth I didn't want to see, or that there was some part of me that I was pushing aside. *I needed to find out what was eating me, so I didn't have to eat it!* My binges were a signal that I was out of integrity and that I needed to look inward before I imploded and sabotaged my life even further. It was time to get to the source of the issues eating *at* me, so I could stop feeding them.

Instead of being something I did wrong, I learned to see my impulse to binge as the prelude to my next breakthrough—a flashing light announcing, *Warning! Something is off! Immediately tune in to your Integrity Alignment Monitor and determine what is going on with you.*

Decipher Your Form of Self-Sabotage

Jane was a self-proclaimed master at self-sabotage! Like a magician doing a card trick might say, "Pick a card, any card!" for Jane it was, "Pick a form of self-sabotage, any form!" Her forte was lying. From as far back as Jane could remember, she lied about pretty much everything. When she was six years old, she told some kids in the playground that her dad had a heart attack. When she was twelve years old, she told her teacher she had a brain tumor. When she was sixteen, she told her boss that she had been kidnapped. When she was twenty-four, she told her boyfriend she had founded a nonprofit and got him grants so that he could live the life of his dreams. These deceptions would always last awhile and then end in a horrible, heart-wrenching explosion of truth when the lie couldn't be sustained.

The theories of the cause of her lying changed over the years. Early on, therapists thought she was precocious—too smart and creative for her own good and bored by regular life. Later, therapists concluded that she was trying to give voice to the emotional pain of her strained family life. Jane's parents divorced when she was young, and Jane's mother abandoned her and her two sisters. Other therapists tested her for personality disorders and sociopathy. Her therapists couldn't help her because she'd lie to them, too, and tell them what they wanted to hear.

For Jane, lying was a way of getting love and approval. She would say anything or do anything to gain temporary and fleeting admiration. Pursuing this insatiable need drove her to create endless situational personas. She was a human chameleon, becoming whatever she thought would make people love her. The only problem was that when people finally *did* love her, she thought that they loved a version of her that she had made up and not the person she was. So her suffering, pain, and yearning escalated.

From an early age, Jane learned to manage the discomfort of being so out of integrity by engaging in other forms of self-sabotage. The backpack she carried around looked like she had robbed a convenience store—it was filled with white wine spritzers, bags of Doritos, and Reese's Peanut Butter Cups. Jane consumed massive amounts of food and developed irritable bowel syndrome from her poor nutrition. She knew she was in trouble and would sometimes pause her binges long enough to search eating disorders on the Internet or buy the newest self-help book. It didn't matter—the food and the lies prevailed.

After college, Jane was fired from her first three jobs because of her lies. Her personal life wasn't much better. She tried to have relationships but couldn't sustain the deceptions she inevitably created. She would lie to some men and tell them that she liked S&M but then feel humiliated when they had sex, and with others, she would pay for everything to keep them around. She had an affair with a married man; they kept their relationship secret, and Jane pretended to be friends with his wife.

One of Jane's greatest deceptions occurred because her lies got expensive. One day, when her father was out of town, she went to his house and found his checkbook. With a shaking hand, she forged her father's signature, drove to his bank, went to the teller, and cashed his check for $14,000.

When her dad came home three weeks later, she realized that she had a choice. She could drive to the Golden Gate Bridge and commit suicide, or she could drive to her father's house and confess what she'd done. Jane's survival instinct won out, and she found her way to her dad's house. When Jane told her father what she had done, he began to cry. It wasn't the first time she'd seen him cry because of one of her deceptions, but she promised herself that it would be the last.

That is when Jane signed up for The Shadow Process. During the workshop, she realized that the biggest lie was the one that she told herself about herself. Because of her mom's abandonment, Jane had decided that she was bad, unlovable, broken, and totally flawed. She believed there was something inherently wrong with her and that seething, black, toxic goo was where her heart should be. During the workshop, she began to realize that when she cleared away the goo, she found a scared little girl looking for love. She also recognized that although she lied, truth existed within her. She realized that if she wanted to live in truth and find peace, she'd have to unravel all the lies—the ones that she told others and the ones that she unconsciously told herself.

Layer by layer, Jane started dismantling her self-sabotage.

First, she stopped drinking. Binge eating was more difficult to stop because she had been using that to distance herself from her lying since she was young. Yet, once Jane became present to the "blessings of her binges," she realized that her relationship with food was a tremendous gift. It connected her with her I AM and gave her immediate feedback about what was happening in her internal world. If something was off with her, she would see it reflected in her food choices. This enabled her to handle whatever was going on in her life.

One day at a time, Jane stopped binging. And when she stopped binging, she became unable to tolerate the discomfort of telling overt lies. Since it was such an ingrained habit, she asked her friends and family for permission to withdraw anything she said at any time by saying, "That was a lie." And her conversations were interrupted with that statement for almost a year as she trained herself to speak the truth.

As Jane continues to realize the advantage of living in her integrity, she continues to explore her next level of truth, which is to step into the person that at her deepest level she knows she can be.

Like our denial, resistance, and excuses, many of us try to justify our self-sabotage. We minimize it by qualifying it. *I only eat junk food on weekends. I only overspend when it comes to self-care. I only have unprotected sex with people I know. I only cheat on my spouse or gamble when I go to Vegas. I only don't set boundaries when it comes to close friends and family.*

Well, it only takes one situation in your life to ruin your entire life. Think about the politician whose career came to an end because of their sexual escapades, the celebrity who no one wanted to work with because of their erratic behavior, or the athlete stripped of their titles and endorsements because they took steroids. If that's not self-sabotage, I don't know what is.

The areas of your life that have any static in them, or where you keep "messing up," are there to teach you, to show you that there is an integrity issue. This may be in the area where you are messing up, or it may be in an entirely unrelated part of your life. Don't be fooled. You could be self-sabotaging in your work life because something is wrong in your life at home. You could be overspending and sabotaging your finances because something is off with your health that you are trying to sublimate.

Your impulse to binge is a warning sign from your I AM that something needs your attention. So instead of beating yourself up, or indulging in your self-sabotaging behavior so that you can prove to yourself how unworthy, bad, or damaged you are, recognize that your impulse to binge can be the catalyst for either your next downward spiral or your next evolutionary leap. This is not a time to shut down. Instead, it is an opportunity to ask, *What's going on?* and understand what your soul is hungry for.

INTEGRITY IGNITER *Find the Blessings of Your Binges!*

What are your favorite forms of self-sabotage? Use a separate copy of the worksheet that follows for each of these forms of self-sabotage and use the following guidelines to complete your worksheet:

How Long   How many days, months, years, decades have you been engaging in this form of self-sabotage?

Cost   What is the cost of this form of self-sabotage? How does it impact you, your ability to show up, and others? Is there a spiral effect? For example, does the lying lead to the drinking that leads to overeating or oversexing/sexting?

Internal Dialogue   What is your internal dialogue during and after self-sabotage?

Excuses   What are the excuses you use to rationalize self-sabotage?

Blessings   Dig deeper, now! Find the blessings. What is your self-sabotage trying to show you about your life or get you to deal with? How could it serve as a blessing or a warning sign? What are the blessings of your binges?

THE BLESSINGS OF YOUR BINGES WORKSHEET

Form of Self-Sabotage	
How Long	
Cost	
Internal Dialogue	
Excuses	
Blessings	

When you find yourself amid self-sabotage, practice taking a moment to stop and ask yourself, *What is going on? What is causing this need for self-sabotage?* Listen to your I AM!

10

STEP FIVE Stop Starving Your Soul

I hope that you've taken the time to examine your patterns of self-sabotage and see them with new eyes. Whenever we hate or resist something, we are pushing it away. We can't learn a lesson from something we refuse to look at. By recognizing the blessings of our binges and identifying how they can bring us to our next breakthrough, we can go deeper. To answer the question, *What is going on?* we must connect within. We must look underneath the BS and self-sabotage and start dealing with the feelings that we drink, eat, smoke, people-please, and work over. It's time to answer a crucial and life-changing question: *What feelings do I need to feel so that I can have a great life?*

What Do You Need to Feel to Have a Great Life?

Most of us have been trained, or have trained ourselves, not to feel. When we experience some sort of hurt, trauma, or pain, we stuff it down. I think of stuffed emotions like time bombs. They become lodged in our body, ready to explode into toxicity and unprocessed emotions. Not wanting to feel or connect with the emotions, most of us stop breathing. Okay, not really, but if you think about it, we tend to go through life either holding our breath or taking short breaths from the neck up. When is the last time you paused and breathed all the way into your belly? Unless you have developed a yoga or meditation practice, you probably go through life with very little attention to the life-giving source of breath.

Why? Why are we afraid to breathe?

Well, to breathe means to connect with our body. And if we connect with our body, we might begin to hear those ticking bombs. We are afraid that if we connect with those internal time bombs, they might explode, that the very feelings we've been trying to avoid will overwhelm us—destroy us—break through those walls we've been erecting for years that keep us safe within the illusion that we are okay.

The problem is that the survival tactics of our wounded ego never work well. The suppressed emotions take up space. And if our external world reflects our internal, and our internal world is filled with toxic goo, then the possibilities of turning goo into gold are slim.

To get back into integrity, we must reconnect to our body. We must unblock the blockages, so we can finally feel the emotions we've been avoiding, discover the wisdom within our wounds, and safely release that which no longer serves us.

Flush It Out

There is a difference between *knowing* you deserve something and *truly feeling deserving* of having that something. The head cannot take us where the heart wants to go. It doesn't matter what you know: *I know I'm lovable; look, I have these people who love me.* It makes no difference if you don't *feel* lovable. Most of us stopped feeling a long time ago. Feeling was too painful. We started to shut off, numb out, and engage in self-sabotage to block our feelings.

It happens all the time: when I ask people if they know or feel something, they hesitate and then reply, "I think I feel!" There is a difference between knowing a concept, understanding it, wanting to believe it, and truly believing or feeling it.

Most of us recreate our past. We marry our mother or father and recreate the environment from our childhood. We live in fear because we know the outcome. And our fear will become our reality unless we go inside and rewire the system. If we don't dissect our emotional pain that keeps us repeating the past, our future will be set in stone. If we grew up with emotional pain, then what do we expect to have in our relationships? If we saw our parents in emotional pain, what do we tend to repeat? The same thing.

No matter what our upbringing, we also develop loaded beliefs when it comes to emotions. We judge certain emotions as good and others as bad. We disown the emotions that we cannot deal with, the ones we are ashamed of, the ones that we were told as children we should not display. These emotions are different for each of us. Some people grew up in households where it was not okay to be angry; some were told they couldn't cry. We were trained, essentially, to cut ourselves off from emotions.

We also tend to disown the emotions that were used against us. If your father often lashed out in anger, you don't want to become him, and so you no longer allow yourself that emotion. If your mother felt powerless and never stood up for you and that caused you pain, chances are you never wanted to feel powerless. For some, having a parent committed to being happy all the time was painful because they could not be authentic or show any other emotion without being chastised that "no one likes a sourpuss" and that they should turn their frown upside down.

As the saying goes, "The only way out is through." No matter how much we try, we can't get rid of our unwanted emotions until we feel them. There may be books on how to get rid of your fear, squelch your sadness, or eradicate your anger, but we will never eradicate these emotions, and honestly, we shouldn't try. We need to develop a healthy relationship with our emotions, so we can be informed and not affected by them, so we can feel them and heal whatever is going on. To be in integrity, we need to get out of our minds and into our hearts—we must own that we are emotional beings.

The blessing of our binges is that they tell us that something is off. They're telling us to look inward, to connect with and dissect the emotional pain that keeps us repeating nonserving patterns of the past. Not only must we take responsibility for what we are creating in the outer world, but also we must take responsibility for our internal world. *We must take emotional responsibility.*

Taking emotional responsibility is about bringing presence and attention to our emotions and determining what is needed to work through them. Our emotions are here to inform and educate us.

Instead of labeling them as "wrong" or suppressing them, we should be fascinated by them. We should see them as a flag that is waving furiously, saying, "Come here. There is something I need to show you." When we recognize that every emotion is here for a reason, or as the great poet Rumi says in his poem "The Guest House," that each emotion "has been sent as a guide from beyond," then we can turn *toward* the emotion instead of having to try to operate on top of it or suppress it. When we stand in 100 percent certainty that ultimately no emotion is bad, good, right, or wrong but is here as a teacher, we will stop needing to avoid it or get rid of it. Instead, we will welcome the emotion, knowing that it has some wisdom or lesson it is meant to deliver. Could you imagine that instead of suppressing your anger, hating your fear, wanting to medicate your anxiety, or trying to cover up your sadness you learned to befriend your emotions, especially the unwanted ones?

It *is* possible, and a certain path to integrity.

When Helen walked into The Shadow Process, she was *so* angry that she could not get angry. She didn't know how to express anger because she had never been allowed to. When it came to expressing herself or any emotion, her voice quivered, and she could hardly speak. She described herself as "the walking dead."

Helen had endured a thirty-year marriage to a man she admitted she didn't truly love. When he left her for another woman, she woke up to the truth that something in her had to change. When she saw a video of The Shadow Process that showed an anger-processing practice that we do, she intuitively knew that she *needed* to get angry. She had a lifetime of rage stored up inside her.

As we began to get to know each other, Helen shared why she was so angry: her father started coming into her bed when she was six; her mother didn't protect her; her brothers went away to college, leaving her to deal with the dysfunction in the house; her father committed suicide; her brothers never came home; and she was left to pick up the pieces and care for her mother who had become a binge drinker.

Helen started dismantling the old beliefs she had around anger. She realized that being told as a child that children, especially girls, should be seen and not heard, had cut her off from her feelings. This was compounded when her father began sexually abusing her. Shutting down was a natural reaction, a self-preservation mechanism of a little girl in a situation that she never should have been in.

During the anger exercise at The Shadow Process Workshop, we give participants an opportunity to express their resentment in an appropriate forum. We let them scream. We let them cry. We let them rage. Nothing is off-limits. It is a space of complete safety and acceptance of this emotion that has been disavowed in our society, especially for women. When Helen's turn came, she knew she could use the fire of her anger to start warming up her stone-cold heart. One by one, Helen pictured the faces of the people who hurt her, and breathing into every violation, wrongdoing, and crossed boundary, she screamed at the top of her lungs. As she released her anger and breathed into the blockages inside her, Helen could go deeper. Underneath her anger were overwhelming feelings of being trapped, resignation, and powerlessness. Secure enough to peel back the layers and tap into memories, some decades old, Helen recalled being two years old when her mother held her down to fasten a helmet around her face and head because of an issue Helen had with her jaw. She remembered the anguish of being trapped inside the helmet. Connecting to this sensation of being trapped and powerless, Helen realized how that theme had been playing out in her life ever since. She was trapped in the bed with her father, in a dysfunctional home, in a dead-end job, and in a loveless marriage.

When Helen and I spoke after this process, she said, "Kelley, I didn't even realize it, but throughout my life, my mother said things like 'Accept your lot in life' and 'You've made your bed and now lie in it' and even 'You shouldn't want for more.'" Helen paused as tears streamed down her face. "I think, under my anger, I felt resigned to my lot in life. I think I stayed with Dave all those years because I didn't think I deserved more. I even remember thinking, well, he will die eventually, and then I'll be free. If that's not resignation, I don't know what is!"

It is a relief to uncover the true emotions we've been running from our whole lives, but it's also hard. What might have happened if we could have dealt with our feelings when we first encountered them? Why do we allow ourselves to be trapped for so long?

Helen knew she could no longer live feeling resigned. She was liberating herself from the prison of the past and taking back her power. In fact, I've had the pleasure of watching her continue to proactively take back her power and achieve amazing things, including healing her previously estranged family relationships. No longer trapped, Helen was named a "woman of influence" in the industry she works in.

Like Helen, many of us are disconnected from our emotions or perceive them as wrong, especially our anger. No one wants to be labeled the negative one. We get blinded by our emotions and don't even realize that underneath them are deeper emotions that can provide us with the nourishment our soul craves.

Giving Voice to Our Emotions

Emotions are signals that something has happened that we need to feel, so we can move on. Because we fear experiencing those emotions, we don't fully process them, which is why we keep repeating our past. Our emotions are there to guide us to our soul.

Our soul craves wholeness and a state of integrity. Developing our connection to our inner world is like weight training: it takes consistency to get stronger. It takes fortifying our muscle of faith and building a bridge of safety between our head and our heart so that we can traverse the path of emotional responsibility, knowing that on the other side of that bridge, our soul knows exactly what it needs. We need to get quiet and be willing to listen because our soul has been trying to get our attention in order to share with us what it needs to feel peace and return to integrity. Your soul may ask you to do one of the following:

- Speak up.

- Set a boundary.

- Accept something for what it is instead of what you would like it to be.

- Slow down, stop doing and multitasking all the time.

- Take some time off or do something for yourself.

- Let go of a relationship that is not serving you.

- Show up in your life in a more powerful way.

- Stop procrastinating and finish the things you start.

- Give up your grudges.

- Live more purposefully.

Your soul is often one of the first victims of the negative self-talking you've done for years. It gets beat up instead of listened to. It gets ignored instead of tended to. It gets left behind while you cross things off your to-do list, as you feed everything but it.

Years ago, when I participated in a transformational program called Evolution Into Mastery, I was instructed to attend an exercise in self-judgment wearing nothing but a bathing suit. A bathing suit!

People shuffled in, feeling exposed and uncomfortable. It's not like we were at the beach sipping piña coladas. We were in a conference room during a self-mastery workshop. Why were we wearing bathing suits?

The group was divided into two lines. We turned to face each other. The role of the people in one line was to give feedback. The role of the people in the other line was to receive it.

Here's how it went. The line of receivers walked up to those giving feedback. Those giving feedback blatantly scrutinized the person in front of them. Then the receivers turned around so those giving feedback could assess their backside. Finally, they would turn again, look the other person in the eyes, and receive their feedback, a word or short phrase about what stood out for the feedback giver.

Then the line shifted to create new pairs and we did it all over again. After getting feedback from thirty people, the roles were reversed, and the receivers became the ones giving feedback.

Yes, this was at first as horrifying as it sounds. Terrified, we all stood sheepishly like we were in front of a firing squad. Originally, the comments stung: "Big thighs." "Cellulite." "Shorter than you look." After a while, I realized that nobody was saying anything I hadn't said to myself, and I was a lot more judgmental and downright mean! I almost had to laugh.

I have gone through this experience twice. There are two comments that I particularly remember. One person called me "an over-the-hill Barbie," which I thought was hysterical since I loved and collected Barbie dolls, and in some way, I took the comment as a compliment! The other remark that stood out was when someone said, *"You're angry!"*

I knew I was angry, but how did *they* know?

That was my first realization that all my "dis-ease," all my emotion from my marriage, was lodged in my body. I started seeing some of my lumps and bumps as unprocessed toxic emotion. The body does not lie. I *was* angry. At one point, I might have wanted to blame my unhappy marriage, my husband, my divorce, or the aftereffects of my divorce for my anger, but I was angry before my marriage, during my marriage, and for a while after my marriage. I needed to stop making my anger wrong, uncover its source, and determine what my soul was craving.

When I did my check-in to see what was going on, I found that fear was always underneath my anger. Fear of financially making it on my own, fear of being alone, fear of not knowing, fear of being out of control, fear of failure, fear of being a bad mom, or even fear of being afraid. The type of fear varied, but it was *always* there beneath my anger. Of course, I had no idea that there was so much insecurity and fear inside me because I had covered it up with my perfected packaging of a woman who had it all together. A strong woman could be angry, but a strong woman could not be afraid. Or so I thought. No one, including myself, would have ever guessed that so much doubt hid beneath my tough exterior.

When I stopped to acknowledge my anger, I finally heard my voice of fear. I took some deep breaths to slow down and connect with it, and finally asked, *What am I so afraid of?* It gladly told me. Knowing that my fear was a benevolent guide and teacher, I felt confident to go deep and ask, *What do I need to do or take care of so I can feel safe and bring peace? What do I need to do to nourish my soul?* Befriending my fear, I learned what would bring me back to a state of wholeness and integrity. My conversations with my voice of fear went something like these:

Kelley   What am I afraid of?

Voice of Fear   Having to pay the stack of bills that are piling up on your desk and taking financial responsibility.

Kelley   What do I need to feel safe, to nourish my soul and feel totally taken care of?

Voice of Fear   Go upstairs, pay those bills, implement a structure so that bills don't pile up on your desk and paralyze you every time you walk into your office. I need you to take financial responsibility.

Kelley   What would be a good structure?

Voice of Fear   Every Sunday, just do it!

✳

Kelley   Why am I so off?

Voice of Fear   You are lonely and are afraid that you will always be alone.

Kelley   What do I need to feel safe, to nourish my soul and feel totally taken care of?

> Voice of Fear   You need to stop isolating, stop pushing people away, and reach out. Go inside, think of three people you would want to be with, and send them a text to see who is available to have dinner tonight.

Determining what your soul is starving for is the foundation of the plan that will bring you back into integrity, the preventative that will stop you from engaging in self-sabotage, and the inspiration that will propel you into your next level of deserving and worthiness.

Feed Yourself First

Paula is what is known as an "it" girl. All her life, she has been considered beautiful, popular, and sexy. She grew up in the Midwest, and when she finished college, she moved to Dallas because, as the T-shirts in the airport proclaimed, "Everything is bigger in Texas!" Paula had a big personality and even bigger dreams. She wanted to make a difference in the world and was determined to make her mark. Needing to earn money, Paula took a job as a hostess at a high-end restaurant. She interacted with many famous, prominent people as she escorted them to their tables. Paula was always drawn to powerful men, and they were equally drawn to her.

Although not proud of it, Paula became involved with a married man. Obviously, they had to keep their relationship quiet. Paula's life became one of waiting—waiting for him to call or show up. She felt enormous pain as it triggered the sadness of when she was a child waiting for her father to come home. Her mother and aunts told her he was on extended business trips. They never mentioned that he had packed his things and moved out. Waiting for her lover brought back the ache of feeling insignificant, unlovable, and unworthy. Unable to stand being someone's mistress, Paula ended the affair.

Next she met David, a celebrity professional athlete. David swept Paula off her feet, and within months they were married. Now Paula was constantly photographed attending high-profile events. Her designer clothing, shoes, and handbags, her fancy cars and palatial home brought her a lot of attention. Even though she loved being in the spotlight as she walked on the arm of her larger-than-life husband, she realized that her light and her dreams were overshadowed by his celebrity.

Paula was living her "fairy tale" and had more toys in her toy box than she'd imagined possible, but she was desperately unhappy with herself and her marriage. She was overspending, drinking in excess, and not taking care of herself. She lost her glow, her passion, and her purpose.

When she started to work with me, it was because she discovered that her husband had been cheating on her. His PR team had tried to blame the separation on Paula. She was furious. Paula made it through the divorce and the humiliation of being labeled a "gold digger." The gift of Paula's fury was that it propelled her to stand up for herself and what *she* had contributed to the marriage. Once the divorce was finalized and she didn't need her anger to fuel her fight, Paula could look at what was underneath the overconsumption and overspending and find her pain and shame at feeling insignificant. Although initially being married to a big man and creating a big life had made her feel significant, after a while, it made her feel small and lost. As we worked together, she became conscious of her deep wound around feeling unseen and disposable that began when she sat on the steps waiting for her daddy to come home.

As this beautiful, powerful woman sat in front of me, I decided to ask, "What are you going to do? Is your daddy ever going to show up? No. But who can show up for you, Paula? Who's going to show up?"

She looked at me blankly. And then it dawned on her. "Me," she said quietly.

I nodded.

"So what would that look like? What would it look like to finally show up for yourself? To finally see yourself and value yourself?" I asked.

Paula shrugged. She had never taken the time to consider that. She had completely lost sight of herself. If she wanted to be visible and significant to others, it had to start within herself.

In a matter of months, Paula took control of her finances, drinking, and all her forms of self-sabotage. She used some of the money that she got from her divorce to go to film school. She now works with abused and battered women and is in the process of creating a documentary about women who lose sight of themselves and their value but reinvent themselves in a whole new light. Now, when Paula looks in the mirror, it is not the designer clothes that get her attention, but the person inside that makes her feel happy and proud about what she sees.

When we ignore our self-sabotage and bury our emotions, we can't learn what our soul is trying to tell us. If you are like Paula, and your soul has been starving, malnourished by filling other people's needs or filling the void within you with a quick fix, some form of instant gratification, or a numbing agent, now is the time to stop and check back in. No one else is in control. You are the only one who has the power to stop your self-sabotage and stepping over your truth and to take responsibility for yourself. What is your soul hungry for? What do *you* truly desire?

This is what living a life of integrity is about—finally taking the time to check in with you. Remember, you are the only expert on you, so take the time to check in! Feel those emotions you've been suppressing and discover the voice you've silenced. Those emotions can guide you back into integrity, back into what you truly want.

INTEGRITY IGNITER *Feed Your Soul What It Is Starving For!*

Start looking at your relationship with your emotions

- Which emotions do you judge as wrong?
- Which are you most apt to express?
- What did you learn about emotions growing up? Not only what you were told, what were you shown? Were certain emotions acceptable and others not? Were any used against you? Did you vow to not express certain emotions? Did you commit to only showing certain emotions?

Now it's time to turn self-sabotage into soul food! Use a separate copy of the worksheet that follows for each of the forms of self-sabotage you identified in the previous chapter. Start with the one that is most pervasive and destructive in your life. Use the following guidelines to complete your worksheets:

Unwanted Emotions   What are the unwanted emotions underneath the form of self-sabotage, the feelings you try to avoid through self-sabotage? Make a list and pick out and star the predominant unwanted emotion.

The Voice of Emotion   Give a "voice" to the predominant feeling that is causing you to self-sabotage. Ask the voice of your emotion the following questions:
- What is making me feel the way I do?
- What am I scared of?

Soul Food   Ask yourself, "What do I need to do to feel safe, to nourish my soul and feel totally taken care of?"

Soul Step   Identify the action step you can take or the structure you can put in place to feel safe, to nourish your soul, and to feel totally taken care of by yourself.

STOP STARVING YOUR SOUL WORKSHEET

Form of Self-Sabotage	
Unwanted Emotions (most predominant)	
Voice of Emotion	
Soul Food	
Soul Step	

Use this worksheet at any time to help you unravel what is going on underneath any forms of self-sabotage as well as to discover what your soul is starving for.

11

STEP SIX Embracing Your Humanity

Do you ever find that you walk around in a state of constant judgment? Do you meet a friend for dinner, and the minute they walk in the door think, *Wow, they look terrific!* Or terrible, tired, tense, or trim? Or when you are "listening" to a coworker, do you start evaluating every word that comes out of their mouth, scrutinizing each sentence, trying to determine what your response should be, the value of each idea, and if you have a better one?

We live in a world filled with "best" and "worst" lists. For many, the magnitude of any moment is based on how many "likes" they receive on social media. Our self-confidence rises or plummets when people we don't even know swipe left or right on our picture. Now, certainly, a big part of being in integrity is learning discernment, what works for you and what doesn't, and what is in your highest interest and what is not. Yet we have on average sixty thousand thoughts per day and 80 percent of them are negative.[1] We walk around judging others and looking for what's wrong. But here's the thing: everything we are judging and deeming wrong in the outer world and in others, we are labeling as wrong inside of ourselves. Why? Because, on some level, we are disgusted by our own humanity. We beat ourselves up for being too much or not enough. Studies report that 95 percent of our negative thoughts are repeated every day. That means we have approximately the same forty-five thousand negative thoughts looping through our brain. And who is this repertoire of forty-five thousand negative thoughts mainly about? *You!*

You and Your "Too Story"

So many people have what I call a "too story." They feel ashamed about the foundation of who they are and, on some level, are always apologizing for being too lazy, too energetic, too stupid, too smart, too curious, too apathetic, too emotional, too objective, too pretty, too boring, too attention-seeking, too big, too small, too talkative, too quiet, too sexy, too asexual.

No matter who you are, I bet that at some point you've been trapped by your litany of limiting beliefs, embarrassed by your essence, and humiliated by your own humanity.

Whether conscious of it or not, we operate from some level of apology, and it permeates everything we do. Think about being late for a meeting or appointment. The minute we walk through the door, we apologize. Or the apology starts before we walk in the door, with a slew of texts saying, "I'm sorry. Running late. Be there in five." Before the meeting even begins, we are in a disempowered position. The initial apology is always followed by a list of excuses meant to justify or explain why we are late. It's like starting in a hole and furiously digging to make your way to ground level.

How are you going to have the life of your dreams if you are constantly beating yourself up? How are you going to live in the light of your grandest desires if you are consistently digging yourself out of a dark hole? How are you going to be your authentic self if you perceive your foundation as flawed or your birthright as blemished?

To be in integrity, we must embrace our humanity by integrating all our emotions, qualities, circumstances, and past experiences. To be in integrity, we must forgive our "flaws." Let's start by uncovering what you are still apologizing for.

What Are You Still Apologizing For?

As I mentioned, most of us have some sort of "too story." People belittle themselves for things like being too unlovable and being a burden on everyone around them as result of their need for love; too cold and unaffectionate and pushing their spouse away; or too irresponsible for getting pregnant at a young age.

When we belittle ourselves, we diminish ourselves. We dumb down our brilliance for what we consider our failings. We cannot be whole and complete if we are minimizing ourselves. We cannot be in integrity if we are belittling ourselves.

Yet since we are all meaning-making machines, we can also weave "too stories" out of positive attributes and qualities and circumstances that most people covet. Although it might seem counterintuitive, when you are in a "too story," the apology can be around being too charismatic, good looking, talented, intelligent, or hardworking, or having too much good fortune or too many gifts. A few years into working with Debbie, I had become an Integrative Life Coach and was doing an in-person workshop. I had learned and worked on many spiritual laws and concepts. I had accepted, surrendered, cultivated faith, and stepped into new levels of responsibility for my internal and external worlds. I had ended my marriage, sold the house I built, and moved. I had learned to let go and embrace change more than I ever thought possible. The day before I went to the workshop, the nanny who had been with me for over fifteen years, who was there when my first child came home from the hospital, told me that she and her husband were moving. At that point, having someone I could trust with my three children was one of the most important needs I had. Feeling lost and sorry for myself, I went up to Debbie, told her my story and my latest tale of letting go, and blatantly said to her, "Look, Debbie, I know that all of the answers are inside of me, but you need to help me out here. What am I missing? Why does the Universe keep serving up situations where I am forced to let go of everything I know?"

Stone-faced, Debbie looked at me and said, *"Kelley, you can't embrace how damn lucky you are!"* I was shocked. It was not what I expected. I thought she was going to tell me about some dark shadow that I needed to embrace. This was Debbie's blunt style directed right at me. Being a bit intimidated by Debbie at that point in our relationship as teacher and student, I didn't ask any follow-up questions. I went back to my room and sat with what she said.

It didn't take long for me to realize she was right.

As I sat in that hotel room, I realized that for my whole life I had been apologizing for being "born in the right bed." I had a father who was brilliant and successful, who taught me how to think and shared his many philosophies on business. I had a mother who was beautiful and had impeccable taste, who taught me about style. I was fortunate to be given the best education, and I was exposed to travel, interesting people, and unique experiences. I was born lucky. Yet even though others may have coveted my lifestyle, as a child I made all sorts of meanings that made me feel ashamed. I felt embarrassed because we lived a lifestyle that was different from how my friends lived. When my mother would get angry at me and accuse me of being spoiled, I made it mean that I was bad and that my having or wanting more was wrong. I was shocked to realize that not only did I have deep-seated feelings of being undeserving, but these feelings propelled me to do more and achieve more to prove that I was worthy of what I was given. I was living from a place of apology that drove me to work harder, downplay and hide what I had, and deflect with humor. And all those years I spent binging on food kept me feeling bad about myself, hiding, settling, playing small—and far from feeling or acting as if I was lucky.

Not only do we apologize for who we are and what we have or don't have, we apologize for events and situations from the past. I've noticed in the last few years that there are more and more men attending my workshops or working with me as clients. I find that many of them, even the most "successful," are still in a state of apologizing, no matter how much they have achieved. It could be for what they perceive to be bad business decisions, not being home enough with their family, not being a good enough husband or father, or some indiscretion. Despite all they may have created, done, or provided, they beat themselves up for their "failure."

I met Alan when I was working with a group of entrepreneurs. For three days, he took in all that I said and asked laser-sharp questions. A CPA who ran a successful firm, Alan wanted a step-by-step equation with answers for how to get from here to there, yet he was unwilling to share any personal information in a group setting. Honoring his need for privacy, we met separately, so he could tell me his story. Alan had been married to Angie for over twenty years. They had four children. The oldest two were in college, and the other two were in high school. Angie's life was focused on managing the children and the house. Alan's life centered around work. They had been coexisting for a very long time. Feeling alone in a loveless marriage, Alan had wanted to get out for years. Yet his wife wouldn't entertain the conversation of a divorce. Wanting to do "the right thing," Alan went through the motions. He ended up having an affair, which lasted for two years. From that relationship, a child was born. Alan came clean with Angie. She was upset, hurt, and outraged. Feeling total remorse, tremendous guilt, and "dirty," he begged Angie for forgiveness and promised to give up the other relationship and stay in the marriage. Angie also made him promise that he would not have anything to do with the child and that they would never tell their four children about this sibling. Seven years passed.

During that time, Alan lived in "Angie Hell." They did not have sex and weren't intimate. She would not go with Alan to see a therapist or do any sort of marriage counseling. He had kept his word about not seeing his other child and felt haunted and tremendously guilty about that. He also lived in fear that someone would find out and tell one of his other children, leading them to hate him for lying for all these years.

Alan was imprisoned by his perception that he was "too guilty" to move on from his marriage, yet his marriage was giving him nothing. He stayed because of the mistake he made and because he felt he had to pay the price.

Alan had apologized again and again. He had asked for forgiveness. Angie had supposedly granted it.

I looked at Alan, and I said, "So what are you still apologizing for?"

Alan looked at me confused. And then it was like a light bulb went off. He didn't have to stay in this small, belittled, guilty space. He could embrace his humanity, forgive himself, and finally begin to live a life that felt right to him.

Cultivating Compassion

We've got to understand that just because we did something that we view as "wrong," that doesn't make our entire existence "wrong."

Once we recognize that what we did is not all of who we are, we will understand that it's not personal and that we are all operating from our wounds. When we can see that the little child inside us wants to be loved and treasured, we can cultivate compassion for ourselves and those around us. Then we can stop beating ourselves up, and we can find the next level of acceptance of our humanity.

We must learn to have compassion for ourselves. Cultivating compassion is the key that unlocks the door from imprisoned to empowered. For every event in our life, for every quality we possess, for every circumstance of our birth, there are a range of interpretations—most of them, as I've discussed, are thoughts not truths, and fictions not facts. None of these interpretations are good or bad, right or wrong, but they will leave you feeling either imprisoned or empowered.

Your meaning-making machine is a narrative of negatives, constantly screaming, *You are not as good as you should be! The past should not have turned out that way! That person did not act as they should have!*

It is constantly beating up that child inside us, but doesn't that child deserve to be loved? Doesn't that child deserve to be forgiven, to come out and play, dance, and enjoy life?

How much longer does that child need to keep apologizing? How many more times do they need to say, "I'm sorry," or prove they are sorry by dimming down their light or joy? Do they deserve another whack from the meaning-making machine?

It is time to treat yourself like someone you love!

It is time to embrace your humanity, to realize that child was doing the best they could—and so is the adult! You cannot move powerfully forward into your grandest vision if you are lugging around a barrel of burdens, blemishes, and blame.

Remember, integrity is about wholeness—owning everything, integrating all that has transpired, so you can use it all and claim your completeness! To become complete, you must find compassion and forgive. Forgiveness requires accepting every situation as it occurred and to surrender any attachment, desire, or opinion that the situation ought to be different.

To release yourself from the prison of the past and the paralysis of pessimism, you need to find the gift of the situation, circumstance, or quality that you are beating yourself up for. If you are living in faith knowing that everything is happening for the evolution of your soul, then you must find the gift so that you can unwrap the wisdom of the experience. Finding the gift is a choice and a practice. But if you don't make the choice to find the gift, then every situation in your life will have the power to use you instead of giving you the ability to use it for your edification and growth. *Remember, life is not happening* to *you, it is happening* for *you.*

In that hotel room, many years ago, when I realized what I was apologizing for and developed compassion for the little girl who felt ashamed and undeserving, I understood that I had two choices. I could continue to feel remorse, settle, sabotage my dreams, and play small because I felt guilty for being given so much. Or I could understand that everything is as it should be, that there is a divine design, and that there are no coincidences. That understanding allowed me to realize I was born in that bed for a reason. That I was put in that situation (that family, that household, that upbringing) as well as all the others (my marriage, my diet struggles, The Shadow Process) for a reason—a reason much bigger than I was. When I opened up to the vastness of the Universe and the miracles that exist in each moment, I understood that I was here to be of service to others! *Who knew?* I went from living in a state of apology and having to prove myself, to wearing a necklace with a charm that says, "LUCKY."

When Alan was able to shift from the eyes of condemnation to those of compassion for himself, he found the gifts in what he was apologizing for—his affair. He realized that in his affair, he experienced something he had never felt before, unconditional love and acceptance. He experienced intimacy and fun in a relationship, something he had not seen in his parents' marriage and certainly not in his own. He also knew that his child was a gift, a gift for the world, and a gift for the woman who got to be a mother. He reached out for the first time and began a relationship, introducing that child to his other children. Now that he had no integrity issue impeding everything else he tried to accomplish in his life, he was liberated.

Our greatest apologies often lead to our grandest openings. As time goes by, and we continue to cultivate the practice of choosing empowering interpretations over imprisoning ones, we can release ourselves from the bondage of the past. The gifts keep on giving as we celebrate our humanity!

INTEGRITY IGNITER *Embrace Your Humanity!*

Identify the situations you are still apologizing for. These may be qualities you are judging in yourself, the negative narratives of your meaning-making machine when it comes to one of your "too stories," or some incidents from the past.

Use a separate copy of the worksheet that follows for each of these situations and use the following guidelines to complete each one:

What Are You Still Apologizing For?   What about the situation are you still beating yourself up for or wishing was different?

Gifts   Find the gift or gifts in the situation. How did that situation, exactly as it played out, benefit or serve you? What did it teach you? How did it make you the person you are today?

Compassion   Cultivate compassion for yourself. How can you see that you did the best that you could at that time and in that circumstance? Despite whatever happened during or because of that situation, why do you still deserve love, self-forgiveness, and to have a great life?

Possibilities   How would you or others benefit if you embraced what happened and let go of the past?

EMBRACING YOUR HUMANITY WORKSHEET

Situation	
What You Are Still Apologizing For	
Gifts	
Compassion	
Possibilities	

12

STEP SEVEN   The Power of I AM

This is the final part of the Integrity Process. This is when we truly begin to tap back into our whole being. To own that we have everything we need inside us, to live a life that is in alignment with our deepest truths and grandest desires, we must step into the power of I AM.

If our outer world reflects our inner world, to create all that we desire in our external world, we must own the entirety of who we are internally. It goes back to Newton's third law of motion that says, "For every action, there is an equal and opposite reaction." If you are owning only 25, 50, or 75 percent of all of who you are internally, then that is what you will be able to manifest externally. The good news is that you already have everything you need—all 100 percent! Every quality and every emotion is inside you.

Let's face it; if you don't feel whole and complete inside, how can you feel worthy, deserving, and full enough to live in your deepest truths and grandest desires?

Think about it. Will you be able to write your first novel if you don't own that you are brilliant and have something important to say? Will you be able to take time for yourself, set boundaries, and say no if you don't own that you are selfish? Will you be able to make that first move when you see someone who catches your eye if you don't own that you are desirable?

If you don't see yourself as abundant, then you won't be able to create abundance. If you don't see yourself as lovable, then you won't manifest love. If you don't see yourself as deserving or capable, then neither will anyone else. To live an integrity-guided life, you must claim that everything you need is inside you.

You don't need to be "fixed," or earn another degree, certificate, or promotion. You may not have recognized or embraced all these qualities inside yourself, but they are there. When you are inwardly focused, when you take the time to know yourself and love all of yourself, not just *parts* of yourself, you want for nothing because you realize you are everything, and thus you have everything you need. Just like your Integrity Alignment Monitor, it is all installed at birth! *You* must bring it to light!

For years, I have guided people as they integrated their shadows, the qualities and emotions that they deem light or dark, good or bad, positive or negative. When we make peace with these qualities and emotions, when we embrace them and unashamedly and unapologetically claim, "I AM that!" then things in our external world will shift, change, and thrive. To truly live a life of integrity, we must do shadow work!

Shadow 101

We are all born in perfect integrity. We are whole and complete. Think about an infant—at any moment they can go from cooing to kicking, from laughter to tears, and from being totally dependent to entertaining themselves. They have access to and can be totally self-expressed about who they are and how they feel. Yet as these unencumbered newborns begin to experience life, encounter events and situations, take in the thoughts and messages of those around them, and absorb the environment in which they are being raised, they start to make meanings and interpretations of all the circumstances. We've seen the impact this can have. One by one, we start disowning aspects of who we are, compromising our birthright of wholeness. This wounded child then becomes the one driving the show, causing us to act out. Our temper tantrums are the result of us wanting what we once had, total possession of all parts of ourselves.

> We spend our life until we're twenty deciding what parts of ourselves to put into the bag, and we spend the rest of our lives trying to get them out again.
> ROBERT BLY[1]

Often the specific events, as well as the meanings we make, fade and live in the shadows of our consciousness. Yet just because they are "out of sight," does not mean they are "out of mind." These beliefs are entrenched in our unconscious mind, which is infinitely more powerful than the conscious mind. These beliefs and meanings are so strong that they tend to drive our behavior, decisions, choices, patterns of self-sabotage, and limiting thoughts. They wield enormous power over our life. They determine what we are or are not able to create, the quality of our relationships, the amount of abundance we experience or suffering we endure, as well as how much success we will enjoy or failure we will be doomed to tolerate.

Our shadows are formed from the following:

- The messages we received from others

- Interpretations we made

- The environment we were brought up in

- Experiences we encountered

- Beliefs of others we were taught or adopted

- What we were praised for or made fun of

- What we saw praised or made fun of in others

Because external input leads to internal meaning-making, we start turning and twisting ourselves around. We disown or hide parts of ourselves.

We learn to hide our light as well as our dark.

Perhaps you learned from your parents that it was not okay to be successful or stand out. You were told, "Don't be too big for your britches" or "No one likes a show-off."

Perhaps no one told you that outright, but you had experiences that led you to unconsciously decide that it was not safe to stand out, be visible, or be great. Perhaps you were a child who was the "star" of the family and your siblings got jealous because of all the attention you received. You unconsciously concluded that "others will be hurt if I succeed" and disowned your light. Or maybe you were the child who was the best player on the team, and at a pivotal moment in the big game, made a mistake. You decided, "I will disappoint others if I shine."

Living in integrity means you own that *everything* you need is within you. Within you is success, as well as failure. Within you is kindness, as well as meanness. Light and dark, dark and light—there is a time and place for everything, and when you own it all, you finally can *choose* when to use each and every part of yourself.

Owning a positive trait that you have denied or didn't see in yourself often feels scary because it requires you to leave all your stories and excuses behind. For some, it feels preposterous to embrace certain characteristics that contradict external reality. For example, it may be hard to embrace "successful" if you are in debt. It may feel challenging to embrace "lovable" if you are alone. And for me, like many others, it may feel like a real stretch to embrace "skinny" when you have always had body issues or the scale says a number that you don't define as skinny. But as Debbie explains in her book *The Dark Side of the Light Chasers*, "If you don't own the skinny person within yourself, he or she will never be able to come out. If you're single and want to be married, you'll have to embrace your married aspect."[2]

When we don't own a trait within us, we lose access to it. Not honoring all of who we are causes us to be out of integrity with our whole self. To get back into integrity with our whole self, we must live in the foundational knowledge that within each of us is everything we see in the outer world—that we are in the world and the world is within us. Every trait or emotion we see in others is within us; the question is, *Do you have access to it?*

To gain, or I should say *regain*, access to a characteristic, we must first uncover the trait we have disowned. With both positive and negative traits, the way to tell if they are disowned is to see if you are simply informed by the existence of that trait in someone else, or if you are affected by it. Does the presence of that trait incite you or excite you? If it is a negative disowned trait, it will incite you and push your buttons. You will be triggered by how cruel, weak, lazy, or irresponsible someone is. If it is a positive disowned trait, it will excite and inspire you. You will be in awe of someone's courage, discipline, or confidence.

Next, you want to be able to own it, to see it in yourself. Bring it back from the dark recesses of your personality. Try to remember how you might have displayed that trait in the past, or if you cannot see that, then how you might display that quality in the future. Remember, every trait was installed at birth, you just lost sight of some, so now it's time to recognize them again in yourself. To get to the place of seeing "I AM that!" you need to be able to see how you *have* that!

The next, and what I believe is the most crucial piece in being able to integrate a quality, is to be able to embrace it. We do that by finding the *gift* of the quality—to recognize how that quality has or could serve us if we needed to call on it and use it. Consider these examples:

- Wouldn't it serve you to be selfish if you needed to create boundaries or take some time for yourself?

- Wouldn't it be a positive for you and all of those around you to have a healthy relationship with your anger, instead of stuffing it down and having it come up as rage?

- If you could accept that everyone, including yourself, is irresponsible, would you still feel the need to always take care of everyone and everything, or would you be able to give yourself a break, take some time off, or do something for yourself?

- If you could allow yourself to be needy or weak, would you be able to ask for help or be vulnerable, and wouldn't that be a nice change as opposed to having to do it all yourself?

- Wouldn't it serve you, the people close to you, and the entire world if you were to own your brilliance, humor, confidence, or joy?

It's as if we all have tools in a toolkit, but we can use only the ones we have access to. To gain access, we must find the gifts of each quality. Now, some people become concerned that if they embrace a quality, it will take over like a tsunami. But that is not the case. For example, if you embrace "mean," you won't be walking around like a monster 24/7. However, if you need to be mean, to defend yourself or say no, you will have access to it. You will be able to take it out of your toolkit, use it, and put it back when you are finished. Without access, you lose the ability to choose. The power of I AM is that it gives us choices.

Who Am I Really?

Samantha was an only child whose parents split up when she was seven. As a young girl, she did not have the mental capabilities to understand that her parents' divorce was not about her. In her child's mind, she was the reason they broke up, and it was because something was "wrong" with her.

Samantha lived with her mother, who was mentally ill, and was embarrassed that her family was not like the other families at the private schools she attended all her life. She tried to fit in, but she always felt that something was wrong with her, just like her mother, and that she was "different," so she turned to drugs, drinking, and sex. Sex became her escape and the fix that would make her feel desirable, if only for a short time. She had several flings with men. On one occasion, she found herself attracted to a woman but would not allow herself to pursue her interest because she did not want to be "different."

Samantha went to college, established a career as an event producer, and eventually met and married Jim. Jim was very different from anyone Samantha had ever dated before. This was the first time she felt totally seen by a man. Further, he loved and accepted everything he saw in her. Reflected in Jim's eyes, there was *nothing wrong* with Samantha.

It didn't take long for things to deteriorate. Jim became needy. He insisted Samantha cook for him and iron his clothes, and if she didn't, he would accuse her of not loving him. Samantha wanted out of the marriage, but they had given birth to a son, and Samantha could not bear exposing him to the pain and shame of being different from all the other children, so she stuck it out.

One day when she was playing in the park with her son, Samantha met a German woman whose daughter was playing there as well. Always intrigued by foreigners, Samantha was drawn to this woman. Although she tried to deny her feelings and the sexual attraction she was experiencing, when the German woman's daughter mentioned to Samantha that her mother was a lesbian, Samantha couldn't deny what was happening. One weekend when Jim was away on business, Samantha and the woman were intimate. Not wanting to be out of integrity in her marriage, Samantha told Jim what happened. Jim became enraged and told Samantha that something was wrong with her if she wanted to break up her family and be with a woman. He said that she would be hated and their son ostracized for having parents who were divorced and a mother who was different.

Not wanting to be different or a lesbian, Samantha gave up her relationship with the German woman and went into therapy with Jim to work on their marriage; she did not want to break up her son's family. But therapy couldn't fix things, and Samantha and Jim eventually separated.

Before long, Samantha met Lyn, and they connected immediately. Lyn was comfortable with her sexuality and had a hard time with Samantha still not accepting her own. Samantha's wounds of not wanting to be different and believing that something was wrong paralyzed her. She couldn't move forward with her divorce, and she couldn't truly move forward with Lyn, a person she loved. She felt alienated from her other friends and family because she did not think they'd be able to understand the experience she was having with Lyn. She felt the intense shame of having a life that was different. Lyn became fed up with Samantha's inertia and moved on.

This is when Samantha began doing shadow work.

One of the first things Samantha needed to do was to embrace the part of her that was different. She had to access that little girl who felt ostracized and afraid of standing out, and own that being different could be a gift. What if being different made you unique and exceptional? Couldn't that be a good thing?

Samantha had to look at how she only had one life, and her son would have his own story. By trying to protect him from the pain she had gone through as a child, Samantha wasn't allowing herself to be loved or lovable, in touch with her true and honest desires.

In a matter of months, Samantha had made huge changes in her life, embraced all of who she truly was, and was finally living in integrity. She looked lighter, happier, and full of love after gaining access to parts of herself that she had been hiding for years.

What are you still hiding? What do you need to bring to light? What would it be like if you could access your entire toolkit, without shame, fear, or frustration?

Believe me, it is a waste of time and energy trying to get rid of the parts of yourself that you do not like or have deemed as "wrong" or "inappropriate." One of my favorite sayings is that God, or the Divine, did not give us any spare parts! Our little-child self did not know that! But it's time to grow up, embrace the power of I AM, and realize and revel in all of who you are meant to be. It is time to step into the brilliance of your wholeness and to be in integrity with all of who you are, feel, and can be.

INTEGRITY IGNITER *Ignite the Power of I AM*

Find the gold in the dark. List seven "negative" qualities that you have disowned in the worksheet that follows. To aid you in this exercise, think of people you dislike, judge, or don't want to be, as well as the qualities you dislike, judge, or don't want to see in yourself. Use the following guidelines to complete your worksheet for each "negative" quality:

Own How have you displayed or could you possibly display this quality?

Embrace What is the gift of the quality? How could it serve you or benefit you?

Integrate What is an action step you could take this week to integrate this quality?

THE POWER OF I AM "NEGATIVE" QUALITIES WORKSHEET

"Negative" Quality	Own	Embrace	Integrate
1			
2			
3			
4			
5			
6			
7			

Ignite your light. Now identify seven "positive" qualities that you are not presently owning. These are the things you don't see in yourself, that you admire in others, or wish you had. List these in the worksheet that follows and use the following guidelines to complete your worksheet for each disowned quality:

Own   Describe a time in your life when you displayed this quality.

Embrace   Why it is imperative that you integrate and have access to this quality now? What is the gift of this quality? How could it serve you? What would you have more of or what would be different if you had access to this quality?

Integrate   What is an action step you could take this week to integrate this quality?

THE POWER OF I AM "POSITIVE" QUALITIES WORKSHEET

"Positive" Quality	Own	Embrace	Integrate
1			
2			
3			
4			
5			
6			
7			

Take a moment to read back through your list of "positive" qualities and breathe each one in, saying, "I AM . . . !"

part 3
THE INTEGRITY PLAN

13 Integrity in Action

Until this point in the process, you have been doing a lot of internal work. You have looked at your past and examined the environment you grew up in and the messages you received to uncover and reveal the meanings you made. You have been acknowledging where you are and how you are feeling, accepting what is, and dismantling your habits, patterns, excuses, thoughts, and beliefs that keep you out of integrity. You have reinterpreted undigested feelings, qualities, and events to find the Divine in the undesired and the wisdom of your wounds. It is all very important work—but we're not finished yet!

Sometimes people get stuck in what I call the "unconcealing" phase. Needing to dig deeper becomes the excuse for not acting. They become paralyzed by or during the processing and don't turn *aha!* into action. As someone who is dedicated to shadow work, I am a big believer in bringing light to the darkness and acknowledging what is keeping us stuck, limited, or in pain. Yet, even when we acknowledge our "stuff," if we don't act, our lives likely won't change much. That's where the Integrity Plan comes in—in this part of the book, I'll guide you from inner reflection to outer responsibility.

Remember that my definition of integrity is "owning all of who we are and living in alignment with our deepest truths and grandest desires." The work we have done up to this point is about owning all of who we are. Now it is time to move on to the next part in the integrity equation. To live a life of integrity, we must step up to the plate and own that we are the co-creator of our life! You must ask yourself, *What do I want? Who do I want to be? What is my deepest truth? What is my grandest desire?*

Just as you can't get to where you want to go until you admit where you are, you can't get to where you want to go until you know where you are headed!

The Soul Line Is the Goal Line

As you move into this part of defining your deepest truths and grandest visions, remember that your psyche is brilliant! It is filled with wisdom to guide you so that you can do and be all that you have ever desired. The dreams and visions you have, whether conscious or dormant, are within your reach. If they weren't, you wouldn't have them, and they wouldn't be *your* dreams.

To live a life of integrity, you must define what is important for you in this lifetime. You must connect to your soul. What is its purpose, truth, and vision? The wisdom of your soul has been with you since birth, and as time has passed, it's become clouded over by your negative thoughts, beliefs, and experiences. One of the reasons it is so crucial to own the power of I AM and realize you are whole and complete is that this is the point of reference you want to reconnect with, remember, and create from.

> When you can own that you are everything on the inside,
> then you have the power to manifest anything on the outside.

When you come to recognize all the negative thoughts swirling around your head and can see them for what they are—stories—then you can quiet the noise and hear the declaration of your soul. To live an integrity-guided life, you must be out of your mind, so you can be in your heart and hear the whisperings of your soul.

There is a distinction between the soul's declaration and the ego's. Although not "wrong" or "bad," your ego's declaration, which is generally your wounded ego's vision, comes from what you *think* you need or should be. It is attached to an outcome. Although following your ego's vision might bring you moments of fulfillment or happiness, they are generally short-lived, and before you know it, you are looking for what's next. From that expensive watch to the promotion to following in your father's footsteps, you must learn to distinguish your ego's vision from your soul's declaration and start living according to what your soul truly desires.

Your soul's declaration is grounded in spirit and inspires you—and the world. It is born out of humility, asking for guidance and praying to be revealed. It fills you with a sense of expansiveness, and you can feel that sense of light and growth spread throughout the cosmos. It grows with a knowing that it is bigger than you, it is meant to serve something greater than you, and it is not at all encumbered by a need to make sense or to be attached to a specific outcome.

To discover your soul's declaration, I've created a five-step process that mandates that you **eliminate, ask, align, act, and allow.**

Eliminate

Your soul knows when something is "meant to be" and what is in line with your highest integrity. It lights up like a pinball machine when it feels that sense of cohesion—like when you have found your calling, your soulmate, or the house you were meant to call home. It also knows when something is off, not in your highest good, when you are living outside of your integrity, such as when a relationship is over, a career is no longer fulfilling, a friendship is off-kilter, or some change is needed.

Always wanting to create from a clean and clear space, before you consciously connect to your soul's declaration, you must eliminate anything that is holding you back, incomplete, or doesn't fit. *Integrity is a process of elimination—you need to let go of that which you have suppressed, clean out that which does not serve you, let go of toxicity, and make space.*

To flow freely and powerfully toward the future, you must eliminate anything that might have a gravitational pull to the past or keep you connected to old karma or chaos. It's like pulling out the old weeds before you plant new seeds, washing your face before you put on makeup, or clearing the table before you set it for the next meal. You always want to start with a clean work space.

In the Integrity Process, you did a lot of work on the inside to eliminate anything that doesn't serve you. But just like we work from the inside out because internal clutter creates external chaos, we also need to work from the outside in because external clutter creates inner chaos, which can result in anything from minor implosions to grand explosions in every area of our life.

I always ask three questions when eliminating anything that no longer serves our outer world.

QUESTION 1 What Incompletions Do I Need to Address?

Incompletions are bloodsuckers since they occupy space in your psyche and want and need resolution. Even if they fade into the background of your busy days, something or someone will trigger them, and the incompletion will return to your awareness—bringing guilt, shame, remorse, resentment, or blame. Incompletions can encompass anything from unfinished projects to emails and texts that need to be responded to, appointments that need to be scheduled, conversations that need finishing, and closets that need decluttering. Incompletions need to have resolution or they will rob us of our integrity and imprison instead of empower us.

QUESTION 2 What Do I Need to Clean Up?

Much like incompletions, I am always looking at my life, doing what I call "spring cleaning" to see what needs to get cleared or cleaned up. Things that must be cleaned up may or may not seem unresolved to others, but they feel incomplete for you. They weigh you down because something about the issue still feels heavy. For me, cleanup is usually needed around relationships, and the cause is often undelivered communication. These are the thoughts, opinions, or upsets that we have with someone that we have yet to communicate. Whether it's sharing a grudge you have been holding for years; admitting a truth you have been avoiding; saying, "I am sorry"; contacting a friend that you have drifted away from to let them know you miss them; or reaching out to someone who is suffering, unde-livered communications drain you of your vital energy.

We often lie to ourselves about undelivered communications. We tell ourselves, *They don't matter. They are better left unsaid. What some-one doesn't know won't hurt them. The other person should bring it up first.* These are all excuses we use to hide our resistance or fear, to avoid conflict or rejection, to please others, to go for short-term gratification, or to play it safe. We convince ourselves that choosing harmony over truth will preserve a relationship, but the opposite is true. When we cannot be straight with someone about who we are or how we feel, our relationship will become fraught with integrity issues. Holding on to an undelivered communication causes separation and deprives us of true intimacy and connection.

Anything that is weighing you down can take you down!

QUESTION 3   What or Whom Do I Need to Let Go Of?

Holding on to a situation that no longer serves us is exhausting. Yet it is the resistance to letting go and the struggle to maintain something that we know no longer serves us that is debilitating. Learning to let go is a huge act of courage. I've learned from the many people I've helped navigate change that, after the fact, they wish they had acted sooner! Just like Sheryl Crow sings, "The first cut is the deepest," the first time you let someone go will often be the hardest. But once you realize that despite the heartache, fear, and hurt, everyone survived, it gets easier. Soon you'll realize letting go is often the most loving thing you can do because it restores your integrity and helps make space for that which will fill and light you up.

We all have people in our life who suck our energy, make us uncom-fortable, are unhealthy to be around, or are just not that much fun. Now, of course, if I am standing in the tenets of shadow work, it is important not to discard these people without reflection and to recog-nize that they are in our life to show us ourselves. They serve as mirrors, point out our projections, and reopen our wounds so that we can go to that next level of self-realization and healing. Yet sometimes, after we have done our work and dug deep to uncover the projections and gifts that person can deliver, it might not serve us to still have them in our life. The most important and loving thing that you can do for yourself might be to let a person go. Letting a person go may mean cutting them out completely, or it may mean establishing boundaries. Letting a person go is not a determination of "bad" or "wrong"; it means that they might not be the best person to have in your life right now. Letting a person go does not need to be dramatic, divisive, or done with anger. Instead, it can be an act of love, acknowledging the role they have played and the lessons you have learned from them. It is best to bless them and let them go. And finally, letting a person go does not mean that you must stop loving that person.

> You can love someone and let them go—it is just
> that you are ready to love yourself more!

Bottom line, letting people go is often one of the most loving things you can do. It is a proclamation of how you will protect your energy, a notification of how you will nurture and nourish your soul, and a declaration of what you deserve.

Monica has been my client for years. At the beginning of the New Year, I do a session with her and her two adult daughters to create an individual vision for the upcoming twelve months. Over time, Monica has let her vision be her guide and has manifested many of her desires. Each year, she takes on specific projects or areas of her life, and her life consistently evolves. She created a new home, launched a new business, traveled with friends and family, and developed a nice rhythm in her life.

Monica had a few relationships after her divorce and then was with the same man, Ron, for two years. The relationship progressed naturally and happily during the first year. During the second year, issues started to arise. Nothing seemed to be working in Ron's life, and the serenity Monica craved had become a struggle as she absorbed Ron's energy and witnessed the victim mentality he brought to every moment. Monica had to admit that the relationship would never be what she wanted. Ron traveled for business, and Monica often found herself alone, even on weekends and holidays. This upset her children since they lived in other states and hated knowing she was by herself. Truth be told, they didn't like Ron and his gloomy mindset very much. They felt their mom was so great that she deserved someone who was always there for her and could share a fabulous life. When Ron was home, he liked to watch TV and was happy "hanging around." Monica was a doer, a powerful force. Although she cared for Ron, she knew they were in different places and had different visions of their futures.

Feeling out of integrity, Monica tried sharing her feelings and coming clean with Ron about what was and was not working in the relationship and changes that she needed. Yet, things never changed. Monica began to feel as stuck as she thought Ron was. A few times, when things came to a head, Monica broke up with Ron. Within days he would reach out, tell her how sad he was without her, and before she knew it, they returned to the same patterns, routine, and discord.

During one of our New Year's vision sessions, Monica broke down. It was obvious that each year she had taken on various areas of her life to make them into a "10" on a satisfaction scale. Yet she could no longer deny that the satisfaction rating she would give to her relationship with Ron was about a "4." She knew that nothing would truly change and that she would be disappointed in herself if, in a year, she was still sitting at home alone on weekends and holidays. Her vision for this area of her life was to be in a committed, fun, easy relationship that flowed and eventually led to marriage. Although it was a difficult communication to deliver, Monica felt relieved when she spoke her truth and ended the relationship. She was inspired to live in the possibility of her vision of a relationship instead of in the apathy and agitation of her life with Ron.

For Monica, letting go of Ron was a declaration of self-love and proclamation that she could not settle for comfortable over compelling, or disregard the whisperings of her soul that told her she needed to let go.

By letting go of Ron and eliminating her integrity issue, Monica manifested a new love within weeks, and they spend every weekend on his yacht sailing on a sea of dreams.

⚡ INTEGRITY INSIGHT

Spring cleaning should be done year-round.

- What do you need to eliminate?
- What incompletions do you need to tackle?
- What situations or relationships do you need to address for closure? What undelivered communications do you need to make?
- What situations or relationships are no longer serving your highest vibration?
- Breathe—what does it feel like inside your body as you envision eliminating these issues?
- What would be possible if you eliminated these issues? Would you have more space or joy? What would you be able to create?

Ask

Once you have eliminated the integrity issues that are clouding your vision, cleaned up your internal and external space, completed or released anything that is weighing you down, and let go of that which does not serve you, you have stepped into a place of neutrality and openness. Unfettered from any constraints of the past, you are a receptacle for creativity. Like the artist standing in front of a blank canvas, it's time to discover what your next expression of genius will be. The ego might tell you to paint a painting exactly like the one you did before—the one that was familiar, that others praised, or that sold for a lot of money. Why? Because the ego is attached to a certain outcome. It likes to feel special or attain certain results. The soul, on the other hand, will tell you to *ask*—to ask to be shown what to paint, to ask and wait for a seed of inspiration to be planted. Your soul's declaration is inspired. It is grounded in spirit. It is divinely delivered through "G-mail"—God mail.

Debbie Ford taught me that "humility is the doorway through which the Divine can enter your life." To receive your G-mail, you must be humble enough to *ask*. Ask to be shown. Ask for a sign. Ask to be guided. Ask to receive. At the start of any ballgame, someone needs to put the ball into play. Well, in this "game," it is up to you to put the ball into play and you do that by asking. Things work in mysterious ways when we ask for guidance and plug into the unlimited energy source of the Universe. The ego is limited by what it knows, thinks it knows, and is attached to. When we ask, we transform from limited to limitless. When we put something out into the Universe, we exceed the smallness of our biggest thoughts and tap into the vastness of what is beyond our wildest dreams.

INTEGRITY INSIGHT

Make the time to ask. You don't need to think about what you should ask for. Let it flow out. Ask to be shown, to be guided, to receive. Stand in the certainty that the Universe will provide, and be open to the concept that you may have no idea what the answer will be or when it will come, but trust that it will.

Align

Once you ask, the trick is to listen. *How do you know what you are hearing? How do you know if it is your deepest truth or grandest desire? Is it the voice of your soul? Is it your ego? Is it the ego masquerading as the soul?* It can get a bit complicated. We have all asked for a sign, received an answer, and then not listened, ignored it, rejected it, or totally stepped over it. Why? Because we weren't paying attention, or we were so attached to what we thought the answer should be, what the sign should look like, or even what our heart wanted, that we did not see or hear what was revealed. To recognize the voice of your soul, you must learn to align.

I'm going to show you how to use three points of reference as your guide—a life focus word, a mission statement, and vision. All three barometers will support you in aligning and then staying in sync with your soul's declaration. They are organizing principles that you can wrap your life around.

A Life Focus Word

The first organizing principle is a life focus word. It's the *beingness* you want to live in and operate from. It's that sensation you want to feel when you breathe into or take in a situation, person, place, or event. For me right now, my life focus word is *expansiveness*. If I walk into a room, whether to lease an apartment or conduct a workshop, I breathe into the space to see if it makes me feel expansive or contracted. I do the same with people. *Does being in their presence open me up or shut me down?* Even with projects I am considering or topics I might write about, I ask, *Does thinking about it make me feel open and excited or limited and closed?* For me to take on anything, it must feel expansive; otherwise, it's not in alignment with my soul's directive.

Your life focus word can and should change over time. As my clients mature, they are drawn more toward words like *serenity* and *peace*. If thinking about or breathing into an existing or potential situation or vision does not bring a sense of calm, then it is not in alignment with their soul, and they should pass. Other popular life focus words include *liberation, joy, gentle, compelling, certain, impeccable, exciting, grounded,* and *loving.* Most people don't realize it, but they are constantly communicating their focus word. Why? Because our soul is always talking to us, trying to get our attention. We need to become present to it. Once we identify our life focus word, then all we need to do is follow the feeling and align with the soul's declaration.

INTEGRITY INSIGHT

Discover your life focus word. What is the state of being or overall feeling you most want to experience? Spend time with different words that arise and notice how each feels as you breathe into every cell of your body. Choose the one that feels best, most comfortable and empowering. Also, consider what you want or what you are looking for as you describe your ideal life to others. Ask yourself, *How would it feel to live in my greatest truth and grandest vision?*

A Mission Statement

The second organizing principle to support aligning with your soul's declaration is to craft a mission statement. Like businesses, individuals can have mission statements. Your mission statement is a declaration of who you want to be and what's important to you. It helps you stay in touch and on task. A personal mission statement has four potential parts:

> **What?** What is it you want to do? To create, empower, teach, motivate, inspire, write, draw, live, heal, cure, train, enjoy, or learn?
>
> **Who?** Who are you doing it for? Children, people who are suffering, millennials, leaders, artists, cultural creatives?
>
> **Why?** Or to what end? Why are you doing what you are doing? What is it that you want to support throughout your thoughts or actions?
>
> **What qualities or values do want to bring forth?** Let your life focus word permeate your mission statement.
>
> For example: *I want to teach cultural creatives about consciousness so that new levels of unconditional love and acceptance will be spread throughout the world.*

Personal mission statements do not have to be big or necessarily save the world. They need to reflect what is most important to you. We are talking about *your* soul's declaration here. It could be for a season or a lifetime. Many years ago, when I was in a leadership training, the participants went through a process where, one by one, we each stood up and shared our mission statement. It reminded me of a Miss America pageant where all of the contestants are talking about world peace. Everyone in the room seemed to have grand personal mission statements. One person wanted to "empower world leaders by teaching them to be more authentic." Another wanted to "write stories for little girls to let them know they can do anything." At the time, my mission was "to be an amazing mother for my daughters, so they would eventually develop their wings to fly." I felt that my mission statement was small compared to the others, but it ended up being the most important thing I ever did. That's no longer my mission statement, as my girls are off making their own way in the world, but it was helpful to state that as my mission, out loud, to acknowledge and feel confident in it.

What's great about having a personal mission statement as an organizing principle that you can easily articulate is that not only can *you* use it as a point of reference, but once you are clear about it and communicate it to others, everyone around you can organize around it as well. Not only did I put my children at the center of my life, but my coworkers knew this too. They understood that I couldn't teach a class or attend a workshop if it conflicted with proms, graduations, birthdays, or even final exams. Having my mission statement as my guiding light made everyone's life a lot easier and drama-free.

INTEGRITY INSIGHT

Map your personal mission statement by answering the following questions

- What?
- Who?
- Why?
- What qualities/values do you want to bring forth?

Create a Vision

The third organizing principle that will support aligning with your soul is to regularly create a vision. In the Integrity Process, as you embraced that "shift happens," you took an honest look at the various areas of your life and determined where you were and your level of satisfaction. So, the next questions are these:

- What are your grandest desires for those areas
  and any other significant areas of your life?

- If these areas were all at a "10" in terms of satisfaction level,
  what would they look like? What would they encompass?

- What do you know is waiting and wanting
  to happen or be created in these areas?

Just to be clear, a vision is a desired result, something you want to achieve. It does not have to be set in time, and you do not need to know how you will attain it. It needs to feel in alignment with who you want to be and what you desire that area of your life to become. You won't know if you are out of integrity in any area of your life if you can't gauge it by what you desire. A vision helps you see these discrepancies.

Often, it does not occur to people to create a vision. Some were never taught to think in the realm of grandest desires or unlimited possibilities. Instead, they focus on the tasks at hand, like going to work, doing laundry, attending their child's soccer game, or putting dinner on the table. These people are focused on day-to-day surviving as opposed to thriving. I don't want to put that down at all since day-to-day life is important; creating a solid foundation with all the day-to-day details tends to provide us with the launchpad to propel us from surviving to thriving. However, if we want to live a life of integrity, it needs to be infused with vision.

For many, not creating a vision is a mechanism to protect the ego. On some level, our scared, little ego does not believe we can have what we desire. We don't want to feel the sting of disappointment or the shame of being the loser who messes up again if our vision does not manifest in the way we think or hope it should. We convince ourselves, often unconsciously, that by not creating a vision, we can avoid negative, unwanted feelings. The opposite is true—avoidance of a situation is the glue that keeps us stuck in personal suffering.

In their purest forms, our life focus words, personal mission statements, and inspired visions drive us to let go of the safety of our status quo, to release our outdated behaviors and beliefs. They compel us to make choices that are in integrity and alignment with our organizing principles. They ignite our internal flame, spark our ambition, and illuminate the pathway of purpose.

Act

Once you have defined your organizing principles and aligned with the declaration of your soul, action becomes much easier. Yet many people freeze in the action phase because of fear. They don't act because they are afraid they will take the wrong action. They stay in a place of confusion because as long as they are confused, they have an excuse for not acting; they remain confused and don't choose because they are afraid to lose or to fail. But the good news is that once you align, all you must do is make choices and take actions that are in alignment with your organizing principles; you won't have to worry about getting it "wrong." As I discussed earlier, integrity is black or white. Every choice, action, and nonaction is either in integrity or not. They are in alignment with your organizing principles, your deepest truths, and grandest visions—or not. There is no middle ground. That is why organizing principles make life so easy. If we are making choices and taking actions that are in alignment with our organizing principles, we are on the right path!

Allow

When you have eliminated all that no longer serves you and humbly asked the Universe to direct and guide you in alignment with your soul's vision and are taking consistent actions that are in agreement with those organizing principles, the next step is to *allow*. When you are connected, inspired, and grounded in spirit, then you know that everything is happening for your soul's evolution. It's part of your divine design. Most of us are so imprisoned by our past, living a life dictated by who we were yesterday, that we don't realize that the Universe holds countless amazing and inspiring futures. Every moment contains an invitation to step into one of those opportunities. We need to accept the invitation and receive the possibility of the present. When we *allow*, we step into receiving. I am a firm believer that life is about receiving and that there are miracles dancing all around us in every moment. We are so attached to our need to control—what we think something should look like—or our doom-and-gloom mentality, that we miss the miracle of the moment, and the invitation remains unopened, stamped "return to sender."

To allow, you must trust that the Universe will bring you everything that is in your highest and best interest when you are ready to receive it. It may not be on your timetable and it may not look as you pictured, but ultimately, it will deliver more than you dreamed because the imagination of the ego mind is limited. I love the adage that when you ask the Universe for something, it has one of three responses: "Yes!" or "It's not time yet," or "I have something better planned for you!"

The Allow stage requires that you open your hands and be ready to receive. If you have a hard time with this, you will compromise your ability to allow. Whether it's compliments from a partner, acts of kindness from a stranger, gifts from a friend, or miracles from the Universe, there are lots of shadows that hamper our ability to receive. Not feeling worthy, fear of not being in control, or disappointment prevent us from allowing and receiving. When we close ourselves off from allowing, we diminish the love, abundance, happiness, and magic we bring into our life! We erect an energetic barrier around us that keeps us from attracting all we most desire. When we make receiving wrong and close ourselves off from allowing, we, knowingly or unknowingly, make a wounded ego's declaration that we do not feel worthy and deserving of the gifts that the Universe has to offer.

The first time I attended The Shadow Process Workshop, I sat in the crowd and watched Debbie. I was so inspired! She was so real and funny—she told it like it was. The workshop was not about some woman lecturing from the stage, but a series of life-changing, kick-ass exercises that supported everyone in digging deep and stripping away layers of false beliefs and painful experiences. The level of sharing that people engaged in, as well as the depth of transformation that occurred, was unlike anything I had ever participated in before.

Suddenly, a thought flashed through my mind: *I want to do that! I want to lead The Shadow Process!* At the time, I had no clue what it took to lead The Shadow Process. Truth be told, sitting in that room in July 2002, I couldn't have imagined what would have to happen, the amount of work I would do—the breakdowns, the breakthroughs, the tears, the triumphs, the endings and beginnings, the deaths, births, and rebirths I would have to endure and achieve. If someone in that moment had told me that it would be a ten-year process and journey, I—or at least my ego—would have probably said, "Thanks, but no thanks." I would have run away. Fortunately, my soul knew something my ego couldn't fathom.

When we eliminate, ask, align, act, and allow, our life will surprise us in ways we never thought possible. Like giving birth, there is something awesome about watching someone live the declaration of their soul. Take Jim, for example. The son of a military man, Jim grew up making his bed with hospital corners first thing every morning! Although he was taught to do things by the book, and pretty much did, there was an impulse inside him that longed to put the book away and create his own rules. Jim had an artistic side. He loved to imagine, invent, sketch, and most of all, create. He thought about becoming an architect, but working as a bartender during college, Jim found he liked mixology, as well as the money he made and the people he met.

Although he became very popular where he worked, he felt constrained by the brands that the buyers bought and mixing the cocktails the management dictated. He wanted to have more input in what the consumer ultimately enjoyed, so he said yes when he was invited to join a prestigious restaurant management team, and he rose in the ranks through various positions. Although he then had more authority, after a while, he again experienced constraint. Even though he wrote orders for the restaurants, he was limited by what the purveyors chose to sell, and he grew bored with the restaurant environment. His soul longed for freedom.

When he was twenty-six, he accepted a sales position at one of the largest wine and spirit distributors in the country. Jim became a driving force. He developed solid relationships with all of his customers and was well respected by his peers. In an industry that was dictated by a good ol' boys' club, Jim had earned a seat at the table. With that seat came expanded sales territories, bigger customer accounts, fancier job titles, and steady raises in salary. He loved his work. He traveled constantly. He met and married along the way. Occasionally, a thought would creep up: Am I going to do this the rest of my life? That his father remained in the same job all his life, never ventured beyond or bought the Thunderbird car he always wanted, stayed stuck in Jim's mind.

As Jim continued to rise through the ranks of his company, his life became increasingly regulated. His day was consumed with stacks of spreadsheets, meetings with his executive team, and long lunches and dinners with clients. He was on a plane at least four days a week, traveling 80 percent of the year. This had an impact on his relationships. His marriage ended, and he never had time for family and friends. He was wealthier than he ever imagined, but he had traded his freedom for a paycheck. With the next promotion came the requirement to relocate. Jim liked his new city, new position, and most importantly, his new team. He was shocked when the company restructured after a few years, and his colleague, who had risen within the company and was now working alongside him, was asked to leave. Jim couldn't help but think, *What if that was me? What would I do if they asked me to leave?* The final straw came when he was supposed to have lunch with his father on a Monday and, as frequently happened, ended up canceling because of work. That Wednesday, Jim's dad passed away from a heart attack.

Jim realized he had become disconnected from his soul. It was time to get back in touch! He eliminated that which no longer served him and left his job. He took a few months off and traveled in Europe. He spent many quiet moments asking, *Why am I here?* and waiting to be shown what was next. Aligning with his soul, he knew he wanted to feel free—he could no longer stand checking his phone every thirty seconds or having his life dictated by a schedule and spreadsheets. Connecting back to the child who loved to draw and invent, he knew his soul wanted to create something that didn't exist. Jim took out his sketchpad and started drawing. First, there was a design for a vodka bottle, and then a wine label. Jim knew that this was it! The tapestry of his life was all being woven together.

Jim contacted his partner and friend who had been laid off. They identified a wine blend they wanted to create, found a vineyard, came up with a name, and perfected Jim's label design. They created a marketing plan and called in their sales connection. Because Jim was in a place of *allowing*, the whole thing flowed, and despite having to spend nine months aging, the wine went from sketchpad to store shelves within a year. Jim's cup was full in every way! His soul's declaration lives on the label of every bottle of wine: "Our time is now. Find your passion. Pursue it. Be true to yourself, and your journey. Be honest. Let your heart be your guide. Love freely. Live generously. Laugh often. Raise a glass. This is our time. This is Nuestro Tiempo."

This wouldn't have been possible if Jim hadn't heard his wake-up call. Losing his father made his I AM go off. *You are missing out. You have the lifestyle you thought you wanted but gave up what you love about life. Please, stop stepping over your truth and get in touch with your soul!*

It's never too late. Whether you are thirteen, thirty, or ninety-three, your time is now! To live a life of integrity, we must own our soul and stand in our truth. It is time to act. Integrity in action is more powerful than anything we can imagine.

INTEGRITY IGNITER *Create Your Plan!*

Napoleon Hill is credited as saying, "Whatever the mind can conceive and believe it can achieve." Having an inspiring vision is the catalyst for achieving more than you dreamed and creating a life you love.

Use the following guidelines to complete your worksheet:

Vision I AM Living In   What are your grandest desires for each of these areas? Feel free to enhance the worksheets and add your desires for any others aspects of your life.

Actions and Choices I AM Engaging In   What are the actions, choices, habits, patterns, or inactions you are engaging in that will lead you to your desire?

Empowering Thoughts and Beliefs I AM Listening To
What are the empowering thoughts that you will consciously choose to listen to, as opposed to the negative ones of your meaning-making machine, that will support you in the fulfillment of these desires?

How I AM Feeling   What are the emotions that you will be feeling when you achieve these desires?

The Qualities I AM Embodying   What are the positive qualities you will be embodying that will support you in achieving these desires?

Identify three actions you will take each week that will lead you to your grandest desires, and allow the rest to unfold.

INTEGRITY IN ACTION WORKSHEET

	Vision I AM Living In	Actions and Choices I AM Engaging In	Empowering Thoughts and Beliefs I AM Listening To	How I AM Feeling	The Qualities I AM Embodying
Health, Wellness, and Body					
Home, Surroundings, and Physical Environments					
Finances					
Career					
Friends					
Family					
Community and Connections					
Intimate Relationship					
Personal/ Spiritual Growth and Learning					
Fun, Leisure, and Enjoyment					
Service and Charitable Endeavors					
Life Balance and Flow					

14 The Integrity Protection Program

We are all vibrational beings. Every thought, action, interaction, environment, or person impacts our vibration by either fueling or diminishing it. To maintain our highest self so that we can continue to live in our integrity, be our most magnificent, and manifest our grandest desires, we must protect our vibration like we would a son or daughter or anyone we truly love and are committed to caring for. We must think of ourselves as we would a newborn child. *You are the most precious gift on the planet!*

Most of us treat other people better than we treat ourselves. We are the fixers, the nurturers, the advocates, the martyrs, the people pleasers, the cheerleaders, or the protectors. We declare a no-tolerance policy when it comes to our loved ones being put in unhealthy scenarios, but we accept the unacceptable or endure the less than acceptable when it comes to our own situations. When asked, "What would you advise your best friend, son, or daughter to do when faced with a nonserving situation?" we are quick to give others advice and guidance we'd deny ourselves.

> Although the saying goes, "Do unto others as you would have them do unto you," the reality is we often do unto others better than we do unto ourselves.

But that stops now! Time to put yourself at the top of your to-do list. Just like the adult in the airplane puts on their oxygen mask first, once we commit to living an integrity-guided life, if we want to stay in integrity, we must be proactive about putting structures in place and creating our own Integrity Protection Program.

We must commit to establishing a new set of ground rules—some for you to adhere to and others to communicate to the people in your life. We have all heard, "You teach people how to treat you," and when we step over our integrity, we (either unconsciously or consciously) give others permission to do the same. When we say things like, "Don't mind me" or "I don't matter" or "I don't have an opinion," we are diminishing ourselves. When we try to remain small and not take up too much space, what are we telling the world? From the moment we meet someone, we are communicating how we see ourselves and defining what is and isn't acceptable in terms of how they treat us. Establishing ground rules and structures will help you protect your integrity!

There's a New Sheriff in Town

As you define and enforce your Integrity Protection Program, some of the people in your life may not be so thrilled that "there's a new sheriff in town," especially the ones who have grown to like the old you who did what they wanted and put their needs before your own. They expect you to be the same person you have always been, and your new way of being and operating may be difficult for them to acknowledge, never mind abide by. I remember the first time I told another mother no when it came to chauffeuring her daughter. She was so used to me saying yes that she had to pause the conversation and ask me to repeat myself. She was totally taken aback by my honoring my time and myself in a different way. The same was true when my coaching practice started to fill up. Before that, I had always been available for family and friends, always the go-to person for advice, to arrange a get-together, or buy a group gift. Once my coaching work became full time, everyone needed to understand that my availability had changed. Some of my close friends resented this shift. "Why is it so hard to reach you?" "Why aren't you picking up the phone?" In learning to protect my own vibration, I needed to realize that it was up to me to communicate what I could or would not take on. Before, I had acted out of obligation or my ability to do it all and be a superwoman, but now I had to rethink my strategy and create practices that protected my energy. Realizing the value of safeguarding my vibration over saving the world, I hung up my superhero cape, and learned to say no!

⚡ INTEGRITY INSIGHT

Start viewing yourself as a vibrational being and become conscious of what situations, places, events, and people cause your vibration to feel more or less expansive.

Homeland Security Starts at Home

As part of creating your Integrity Plan, you needed to clean up, clear out, let go, and eliminate that which no longer serves you. It is vitally important that this clearing process becomes a way of life. Look for what or who no longer serves you, drains you, or is the impetus for a downward spiral. For homeland security to be effective, you must create boundaries around anyone or any situation that diminishes your vibration, drains your life force, or decreases your feelings of vitality. Strong, healthy boundaries empower you, turning victim to creator, because they assist in defining what you will or will not do, what you will or will not tolerate from others, and who you will or will not allow in your space. You might not be able to cut all the people that deplete you out of your life or rectify every situation instantly, but you can become aware of who or what triggers you. You can start to devise a plan about how to take responsibility for these situations so that they no longer overwhelm your life, create upset, and become the reason for self-sabotage or not treating yourself like that precious newborn.

Establishing boundaries with others is a common theme for many of the clients I work with. Whether it be with an ex-spouse, overbearing boss, intrusive parent, know-it-all neighbor, gossiping clique, or even an overly dependent child, creating boundaries is an essential part of your Integrity Protection Program. I like the analogy of a house when it comes to creating boundaries. You must be mindful and vigilant about who you allow in and how far. Some people are only allowed onto the front porch. Others are invited into your living room. Some you may welcome into your kitchen. A select few you might allow into your bedroom or closet. Then there are those who are not allowed onto the property at all. The gate is latched and the door is closed! Why? Because they haven't earned or have abused the privilege of being in relationship with you, and you deserve only those who are worthy of your vibration.

Define what is healthy and unhealthy for you. When we honor healthy boundaries, and declare intolerance of unhealthy, we set limits on how much drama we will accept and how far from our divinity we will allow ourselves to go.

> We cannot allow our need for each other
> to exceed our love for ourselves.

People with healthy boundaries give what they can afford and know when to stop. When you focus on that which is healthy to feed your soul, that is what you become!

⚡ INTEGRITY INSIGHT

- What are some healthy boundaries you need to establish?
- What are the ones you need to communicate to others?
- What are boundaries of others that you need to respect?

Border Control

Just like countries need boundaries to maintain security and control the flow of people coming in, we want to be proactive about whom we let into our inner circle. Replace all the integrity snatchers who empower your helplessness with like-minded people who hold you in your highest light and are committed to living in integrity.

> Marry your conscience. Marry the one who
> makes you want to be a better person.
> JAY LENO[1]

Integrity-minded people do the work to open and accept themselves, so they can be more open and accepting of others. By valuing their own truth, they value the truth in others. By owning their own greatness, as well as their humanity and divinity, they can celebrate the greatness, humanity, and divinity of others. Because they are being fully responsible for themselves, there is no projection, finger-pointing, blame, or drama. Integrity-minded people cheer each other on. They love you enough to risk speaking their truth if it will support you in living in your magnificence. They remind and inspire each other to continue to strive for their goals and to be as great as they can be. They are dedicated to each other's visions and will fight for you to achieve your goals even on the days you feel tired, hopeless, or want out. They are there to lend an ear, give advice when asked, and be compassionately ruthless when someone or something is off track. They are your champions and recognize that you being in your integrity is not only in your highest good, but will benefit the world as well because they know that you (and they) are here for something much bigger than yourself.

Surrounding yourself with people who take responsibility for their emotions, lives, actions, and words is critical when it comes to preserving and protecting your vibration. Anything else will feel like babysitting or exhausting. The issue is not about them, but about you. The important question becomes, *Who is best for me to be around?*

⚡ INTEGRITY INSIGHT

- Who are the positive forces in your life?
- Who brings out the best in you?
- Who champions you being your best?
- Who is best for you to be around?

Define Your Top Two

Once you have gone through your life and taken an inventory of the people and situations that no longer serve you and have eliminated them, created boundaries around them, or devised a plan to handle them, you have the time and space in your life for the people, situations, and activities that bring out the best in you.

In the Integrity Plan, we discussed creating a strategy that was in alignment with your organizing principles. But to protect our integrity, we need to be even more vigilant. We need to prioritize. *What are your top two most important aspects of life right now?* If you can't answer that, then you will be faced with commitment issues because your top priorities will end up in conflict. I see it all the time with clients. They think they are committed and hardworking, which they are. But this is where they need to be busted on their own BS. By not prioritizing, and in their attempt to "do it all," they end up self-sabotaging that which is most important. Their attempts to multitask dilute their power to show up for any one thing.

A friend who is also a transformational teacher and leads workshops told me about a new project she was establishing. As she excitedly rattled off her multitiered strategy, she exuberantly expounded upon all the ways I could and should play a role. Being a lover of great ideas, spiraling up in the energy of other people's visions, and of course having my ego stroked by someone telling me how fabulous I was and what "an amazing addition" I would be might have led me to follow along with her assumption that I would be part of her project. However, knowing the importance of priorities, I told her that my focus was writing this book and running The Ford Institute. I could not focus on her project because I had to spend my time on my own! When I hung up the phone, I felt empowered and clean. There was no hemming and hawing, no giving up my power to be a "good friend"—I spoke my truth, and she understood.

To reach our dreams, we must make choices that are congruent with our soul's vision. To make our vision a reality, we must declare our priorities! *What is most important to you at this moment in time?* It could be your children, moving, your relationship, taking care of an elderly parent, writing your book, or finding time to relax and regenerate. You need to take time to make a list of your priorities, rank them, and proclaim and protect your top two. When you use your priorities as your true north and commit to making choices that are in alignment with them, your decisions become clear, and choices become simple. You claim your worth and your position on the top of your to-do list. You are affirming that you are no longer so worried about disappointing others because you can no longer tolerate disappointing yourself! *When you define your priorities, you automatically become your top priority!*

⚡ **INTEGRITY INSIGHT**

Refer to the Integrity Plan that you created in the previous chapter. Of all the visions and desires you listed, determine what your top two priorities are right now. Use them to guide you as you make decisions.

Structures for Success

At the end of The Shadow Process Workshop, we have a conversation about continuing the journey. After spending two and a half days in a nurturing environment where participants can be authentically themselves and share their deepest pain as well as their most magnificent thoughts and dreams, some people are apprehensive about returning to their everyday lives. They have said things and shared stories that they may never have told anyone. They have formed bonds with people they have known for two days that may be more powerful than bonds they have with friends and family they have known for decades. They feel so tuned-in and turned-on by their experience that they are nervous that when they walk out of the workshop doors, these feelings will fade. To support them, we talk about structures for success when they go home, protecting their vibration, and increasing levels of self-care.

Solid structures, like creating boundaries, establishing border control, and identifying priorities, are the keys to the Integrity Protection Program. Don't be afraid of structure—it won't take away your freedom, spontaneity, and ability to control your life. It won't make you boring; the opposite is true. Creating structures that help you manage your life and time, that consider your need to nurture your well-being and your playtime, downtime, free time, and time for friends, family, and fun, gives you more freedom.

Structures are an act of self-care and a demonstration of self-love! They are not all about doing and achieving, although they will support you in doing and achieving more since they feed your internal flame. They are about supporting your beingness and highest vibration. My structures include everything from how I nurture my body, to seeing my children who live in other states at least one weekend per month, to having a girls' night with my closest friends every few weeks, to not going out more than three nights in a row, to Sundays with my mother, to taking twenty-four hours to respond to a request, to daily prayer and gratitude, to scheduling in free time so that I protect my spontaneity to do what I want in that moment. Often, even before I arrange a vacation, I research the area, so I know exactly how I can implement my structures when I reach my destination. From finding exercise classes to hiking trails to knowing markets that sell my must-have foods, I am always good to go before I take off. Why? Because I know what serves my vibration and what does not. When you protect your integrity, you show the world that you value you!

Structures must be in place to also safeguard you from your weaknesses. Now that you are reaching the end of *The Integrity Advantage* journey, you have arrived at a place of truly knowing yourself. You know your weaknesses, your triggers, your forms of self-sabotage. That means you know how to create structures that will prevent temptation. *It is better to know yourself, not test yourself!* Remember, integrity is not about perfection.

Think of the times that you have said, "Just one bite," and eaten the whole thing; attended a "sale" and blown your budget; promised yourself it would be just one kiss and ended up spending the night; or answered the phone after not speaking to your ex for months and were right back in that place of heartbreak or obsessing about them all the time. To protect your integrity, you need to cut out the wishful thinking or the delusions that this time it will be different—that this time you will be able to live with that open bag of cookies or only use that open bottle of wine for cooking instead of pouring yourself two glasses each night until the bottle is finished. Don't test or tempt yourself. Be honest about what you can and cannot handle, and then create structures so that you will not find yourself testing yourself and your resolve. Have a "no alcohol in the house" rule. Delete his number from your phone. Don't go shopping on your own.

There is still freedom in your life, but you know that testing yourself is not worth it.

⚡ INTEGRITY INSIGHT

Start defining your structures for success. Think about what truly serves you in terms of your self-care, how you schedule your day, the people you want to spend time with, all the aspects in your life that fuel your internal flame. Don't just define what these things are, but examine how often you should be engaging them. What is the best way to make them happen?

The "Right Questions" for the Integrity Protection Program

In Debbie Ford's life-changing book *The Right Questions*, she lists ten questions we can ask to empower ourselves in any situation. Asking powerful questions is one of the most effective ways to lead you back to you, strengthen your muscle of self-trust, and connect you with your I AM. In terms of the Integrity Protection Program, if homeland security starts at home, then the I AM is the most powerful weapon you have in your battle for self-trust. I've come up with seven "right questions" that can help with this. They turn angst into ease, as they connect us to our truth and help protect integrity.

1 Who Do I Want to Be in This Moment?

This is one of my favorite questions. Since integrity is about beingness, you can always decide who you want to be in every moment. Do you want to be forgiving? A person who speaks their truth? A person who is known for showing up? That others can count on? That keeps their word? The person who is always kind to others? The person who brings people together?

My youngest daughter is one of my greatest teachers when it comes to this. Believing in holding others the way she wants to be held, she is adamant about not gossiping and judging. If she is in a group where they are talking about someone, she will change the topic, steer the conversation in a different direction, leave the room, or blatantly suggest that perhaps they don't know what they are talking about. She is committed to being a positive presence in the world and uses this question as part of her practice.

2   What Is the Most Loving Thing I Can Do for Myself in This Moment? What Is for My Highest Good?

Since we are creatures of habit, as well as vibrational beings, we want to become present and attuned to what is the most loving thing we can do for ourselves in every moment. If we want to learn what self-love is, then we need to take it on. It doesn't come from the outside. It comes from you learning to fill up your own cup. Using this question helps us to do that. There are days when I let this question lead me. I use it in making every decision, from the activities I partake in to what I eat to whom I spend time with. I am constantly fortifying my I AM and protecting my integrity by honoring this rule: "If it is not a big 'Yes!' then it is a big 'No!'"

3   What Am I Supposed to Be Learning from This?

Radio host and author Tom Bodett is often quoted as saying, "In school, you're taught a lesson and then given a test. In life, you're given a test that teaches you a lesson." At every moment, we have a choice to be the co-creator or the victim. Whether it is a flood in your basement or a flood of emotions from a breakup, life is the most benevolent teacher. To get the gift of every situation and to catapult yourself from imprisoned to empowered, continually ask yourself, *What am I supposed to be learning?*

4 What Don't I Do?

This is a fun question to start playing with. If to know yourself is to love yourself, then a great way to protect your integrity and deepen your self-love is to become clear about what you "don't do." Defining what you don't do supports you in establishing boundaries, and it makes decision making easy because if it is on your "don't do" list, then the answer is no. Here are some examples of things people don't do: drama, gossip, middle seats on airplanes, camping, spicy food, chewing gum, bad hair, makeup to go workout, drive at night, wear rings, eat chicken, text your ex, threesomes, and so on!

5 What Level of Consciousness Am I Bringing to This Moment?

Most of the time, we all seem to be miles away from where we really are. We are either dwelling on the past—trying to make sense of something we will probably never understand, wishing an outcome had been different, overthinking a past situation and wondering, *Why?*—or we're fantasizing, trying to forecast or manage the future. If we are not in the past or future, we are lost in our thoughts, fighting with the negative internal dialogue looping around our mind, or "checked out" and burying ourselves in our favorite numbing agent. It does not matter which of these levels of consciousness we dwell in since, in any case, we are missing the possibilities of the present. Our story will never end differently if we are dragging our past into every moment. Studies show that the happiest people are those who live in the present. The good news is that asking yourself this question causes an automatic change in direction. When you choose to veer off the level of consciousness that you have been operating from and move to a different one, your vibration shifts, your life and the world look different, and there are new choices available to keep you in integrity.

6   What Is My Purpose and Intent?

Up to this point, you have done a lot of work to clear your slate. To sustain this trajectory of truth, you want to keep your actions and communications clear and on point. Often, we are driven by multiple motivations. Our priorities get muddied by multitasking. Our communications get layered with conflicting agendas. Think about the times you were trying to make a point or a request, and it got lost in your need to defend yourself, prove that you were deserving, your need to make someone else wrong, or in some passive-aggressive repartee. Staying present to your purpose and intent aids you in keeping your eye on the prize and in cutting out anything that is superfluous or contradictory. When you stay on point, you make it easier for others to focus. When you show up clear and focused, your trust in yourself and other people's trust in you flourishes because you mean what you say and you say what you mean.

7   What Am I Making This Situation Mean about Myself, My Life, or the World?

Integrity snatchers are real, and since we are human, we are susceptible to all of them. Signing up to live an integrity-guided life does not mean you won't have moments of fear, shame, times when you go into a story in your head, and reactiveness. Chances are, you will get triggered. How will you respond to those triggers? Will you go down the rabbit hole of negativity, or will you use the situation to learn, gain new insight, or own another piece of yourself? This question supports you in uncovering the thoughts that have sabotaged your efforts and exuberance. It aids you in discovering the next piece of yourself that needs owning to keep you in your power and on your path.

Ultimately, these seven questions lead back to your most powerful ally of all, your Integrity Alignment Monitor. Your I AM is at the heart of devising and living in your Integrity Protection Program.

❯ INTEGRITY IGNITER *Formulate Your Integrity Protection Program*

Homeland security starts at home! To live the advantage of an integrity-guided life, you need to safeguard your highest vibration. Use the following guidelines to aid you in filling out the worksheet that follows and formulating your Integrity Protection Program:

Boundaries   What are some of the boundaries that you need to establish and enforce with others? What are some of the boundaries of others that you need to respect and adhere to?

Borders   Who are your champions and cheerleaders? Who are the people and communities that bring out the best in you and are committed to your success?

Priorities   What are the top two priorities in your life at this moment?

Structures for Success   What are the structures that add to your success, support your highest vibration, and keep you on track in claiming and living in integrity? Look at the different areas of your life to help you define your structures, areas like health, wellness, and self-care (diet, exercise, personal hygiene, personal health, beauty routine, rest); spiritual practice (mental and emotional well-being); the people you want to spend time with; and your free time and "me" time.

THE INTEGRITY PROTECTION PROGRAM WORKSHEET

Boundaries	
Your Boundaries to Establish	
Others' Boundaries to Respect	
Borders	
Priorities	
Structures for Success	
Health, Wellness, and Self-Care	
Spiritual Practice	
People You Want to Spend Time With	
Free Time and "Me" Time	

As your integrity and life continue to evolve, so will your Integrity Protection Program. Continue to check in and update it.

CONCLUSION The Integrity Promise

Bronnie Ware is a palliative nurse from Australia who helps care for people in the last weeks of their lives. After several years of witnessing the clarity dying people have about what they wished they had done differently, she compiled a list of what she found to be the five most common regrets they held. The number one regret was this: "I wish I'd had the courage to live a life true to myself, nor the life others expected of me."[1]

This is what the entire journey of *The Integrity Advantage* is about—living a life where we feel complete enough to show the world all of who we are, courageous enough to live in our deepest truth, and confident enough to go for our grandest desires. And if a pang of regret pops up, or those feelings of wanting, wishing, or waiting creep in—and they will because we are all human—be grateful for them. You now know they are signs from the Universe urging you to tune in to your I AM, to see what is going on and what you need to take care of, so you can step back into your truth, loving your life and claiming your magnificence.

> The important thing is this: To be able at any moment to sacrifice who we are for what we could become.
> CHARLES DU BOS[2]

We know that being out of integrity can launch a downward spiral. It can lead to feelings of shame and unworthiness, which lead to self-sabotage and making choices that are not in our highest interest. These can generate greater feelings of being out of integrity and unworthiness, leading to more self-sabotage, and the spiral continues straight into a dark abyss. Yet, the moment you declare, "Enough is enough!" and focus on who you want to be in that moment, the downward spiral becomes a shooting star. Just like being out of integrity breeds more of the same, so does being in integrity, since *integrity is exponential!* It builds on itself. Your I AM guides you to make high-level choices, which fuel your feelings of worthiness, your desire to make high-level choices, and your enthusiasm to rise up in your commitment to living in integrity.

When you operate from this reference point of wholeness, truth, clarity, fascination, liberation, and magnificence, you will find there is no other way to live. Once you commit to living a life from a place of integrity and self-referral, no other way of being will feel authentic or in alignment. It's like when you taste an amazing piece of chocolate or a fine wine, or experience a truly honest heart connection—after that, it's hard to settle for anything less. Once you live *The Integrity Advantage*, that way of being is coded in the consciousness of every cell of your body, and it feels empty, wrong, and dishonoring to live any other way. It no longer works to be run by shame or fear, wear a mask, put others in front of yourself, play small, remain in denial, stay asleep, or do anything that feels unhealthy.

In the play *Auntie Mame*, Auntie Mame declares, "Life is a banquet and most poor sons-of-bitches are starving to death!" *The Integrity Advantage* is about going from starvation to celebration. When we live an integrity-guided life, we no longer need to live in a place of denial or deprivation, stuck in a state of struggle and confusion, questioning or second-guessing every decision. We trust ourselves—to discern which banquet to go to, what delicacies to indulge in, and when to leave the party. The feast-or-famine mentality, which has driven us in the past and eventually resulted in self-sabotage, subsides as we trust ourselves to nourish our soul. Like food turns into energy, trust turns into confidence! You will create more colorfully, play more passionately, love more completely, think more outrageously, act more assuredly, and live more fabulously as you delight in life's glorious banquet of delicious possibilities.

Integrity is the new self-love!

*

I want to congratulate you. By getting naked; busting your BS; learning to shift your meaning-making machine from "I am not . . ." to I AM; integrating all your qualities, emotions, and past experiences by finding the blessings of your binges; embracing your humanity; and owning all of who you are, light *and* dark, you have chosen to know, see, honor, and love yourself in a whole new way. Ultimately, it all comes back to self-love—that elusive concept that people talk about but few know how to reach. I used to roll my eyes at this concept, until one day, I truly experienced it. It was after my divorce. I was working as an Integrative Life Coach and had a thriving practice that totally filled me up. I was committed to helping others across that bridge from fear to faith to freedom. I had traded in my need for perfection for wholeness, and had gone from wanting to wonderment as I lived in the magic of a synchronistic partnership with the Universe. I felt liberated living in my truth and claiming my magnificence. I stood in my office, pausing, punctuating the moment, by exclaiming, "My God, I have fallen in love with myself!" That is my intention for where *The Integrity Advantage* will lead you—to have you fall in love with yourself, again and again!

To love yourself you need to know yourself.

I hope this book has started you on that journey.

My prayer for you is that you keep on a path of self-love, not only for yourself, but for those around you and for the world.

Collective Integrity

I began this book by talking about the trust crisis in the world today. Imagine what would be possible if we all took on being the change we want to see in world. What would be possible if . . .

- We all lived in our wholeness, not worrying or fearing that you had something I did not have?

- We embraced our humanity and had compassion for the humanity of others instead of judging?

- We trusted and respected that we, and everyone
  in the world, had our answers within?

- We felt no need to fight to be right, but could
  graciously do what was right for us?

When you know and love yourself, you don't feel threatened or in competition with others. It makes life so much easier. Instead of being caught up and brought down by the smallness of the wounded ego, you are lifted by your limitlessness. When you value yourself, you can see the value in others, and a culture of respect flourishes. Living in the vastness of the Universe, you hold that vision for others. Not only will you feel inspired and grounded in spirit, but inspiring—as you present the path of possibilities for all.

Living in integrity, you stand as a beacon. Not only does it draw other integrity-guided people into *your* life, but it impacts everyone you interact with and creates an opening for everyone around you. When you can be straight with others, they can be straight with you. Being in integrity allows you to have intimacy, not just with one person as a partner, but with the world. You can be deeply connected. You can feel love for humanity instead of judging, projecting, and holding others responsible for disappointments, dashed dreams, and parts of yourself and your life that you dislike.

> When we each own our wholeness,
> it impacts and strengthens the whole.

When you make a profound shift in your consciousness and in your actions, it creates a ripple effect with the people and world around you. We have all heard the expression, "The whole is greater than the sum of its parts." The level of responsibility we each take for our personal integrity impacts the evolution of the collective.

This is what is possible when we take a journey of integrity and commit to it for life—it is the beginning of anything you want and more that you ever dreamed possible!

Acknowledgments

I am blessed to have the most amazing people in my life! They love, inspire, support, push, challenge, applaud, see, and accept me. They are and have been with me every step of the way, and for that I am truly blessed and infinitely grateful!

The fact is, everyone who has touched my life has impacted this book. Although I couldn't possibly thank them all, my hope is that they know in their heart the love and gratitude I have for them. However, I would be remiss if I did not personally thank the following people:

My parents, for giving me the amazing foundation and education that has made everything possible. To my mother, Eleanor Kosow, for always being there for the girls and me. You are the epitome of what a matriarch of a family should be. You are an icon of style and a role model of strength, moral conviction, and faith! To my father, Joseph Kosow, I wish you were here longer, but I could not have asked for someone who made a bigger impression. Your humor, brilliance, and larger-than-life persona—I am proud to be my father's daughter!

Debbie Ford, for being a brilliant teacher, inspiration, and friend. Thank you for seeing in me what I did not own in myself. "You'll be with me like a handprint on my heart" forever, and "because I knew you, I have been changed for good."* I miss you but know that you are doing your thing from the other side.

Elaine Berkowitz, Cathy Blank, Mayi de la Vega, Claire Faithful, Judy Lefton, Rachel Levy, Jane Marcus, Pauline Merl, Starr Porter, Claudia Potamkin, Laurie Riemer, Millinda Sinnreich, and Lynda Weiser for being the best friends, confidantes, and support system a person could have. Thank you for being aunts to the girls and sisters to me!

*Lyrics from "For Good" from the musical *Wicked*.

Ellen Collier, my first teacher, for holding the space and being the catalyst for so many blessings. I miss your safety and your strength.

Claudette Herbert, for always being there and giving 110%! Watching you evolve into the woman that you are has been a joy! Thank you for all that you do and for your fierce dedication.

Robert Fox, for being so impeccable as a trainer and a friend. I loved our mornings together. Thank you for sharing your humanity and your heart with me. Missing you still hurts, and know "I am hooked forever!"

Gabriel "Stunna" Varona, for being there for me every day, kicking my butt, and understanding my facial expressions and the way my mind works! Who you are and what you bring to the world is awe-inspiring (shoesforstreets.com)! And to my workout buddy, Jill Finkelstein, for always showing up and caring!

Julie Stroud, for believing in me and supporting me in every way. Our partnership and the trust and respect we have for each other are gifts that I truly cherish! I can't thank you enough for your steadfast dedication, brilliance, and friendship.

Fran Fusco, for being my other touchstone and always giving me the space and encouragement to keep going.

All the Integrative Life Coaches at The Ford Institute (thefordinstitute. com), who have supported me, grown up with me, and walked this evolutionary path with me—thank you for sharing your lives, lessons, laughter, and love. And a special big thanks to Julie Bishop, Shari Coltune, Nancy Levin, Bette Schubert, and Vincent Scotto for their extraordinary sharing and support. Your dedication and generosity of spirit have impacted not only me, but thousands. And to my teachers and mentors over the years, thank you for your wisdom, guidance, and feedback.

My clients and all of those who contributed their stories to this book. Thank you for sharing your lives, entrusting me with your confidences, and allowing your stories to be used to serve others.

Michael Mirdad for your guidance, wisdom, and generosity.

The amazing men in my life who have loved, supported, and put up with me. Thank you for all that you brought to my life and taught me about love and myself.

Tom Bird, creator of the Write Your Book in a Weekend workshop (tombird.com). Thank you for creating the space for me to realize that I had a book inside me and giving me the opportunity to birth the first version of this book. Your generosity, candor, and caring was the huge push I needed to make this dream into a reality.

Cindy DiTiberio—if you had not come along, I probably would have given up! I cannot thank you enough for your genius, generosity, structure, true caring, and all that you bring to the table. Having you by my side made all the difference!

Stephanie Tade, my literary agent (and her assistant, Colleen Martell), for having faith in me and supporting me in truly finding and expressing my voice. Thank you for standing with me in my vision, standing up for me when I was insecure, and giving me the confidence to be authentic in unknown territory.

Alice Peck, for your authentic encouragement, generous heart, and brilliant editing.

All the people at Sounds True, for your dedication and commitment to and support for not only me, but also the world of transformation, personal growth, and education. I am honored to be part of your team.

The three most important people in my life, Chelsea, Nikki, and Ryann. I am so blessed to have you as daughters. Beyond being my favorite people in the world, I am in awe at what amazing human beings you are. You are my greatest gifts!

Notes

INTRODUCTION   Stepping Over Your Truth

1. Richard Bach, *Illusions: The Adventures of a Reluctant Messiah* (New York: Delta, 2012), Kindle edition, 48.
2. Deanna Minich, *Whole Detox: A 21-Day Personalized Program to Break Through Barriers in Every Area of Your Life* (New York: HarperOne, 2016), 5.

CHAPTER 2   Integrity Snatchers

1. Brené Brown, "Listening to Shame," TED talk, March 2012.
2. George Bernard Shaw, *Back to Methuselah*, act I, *Selected Plays with Prefaces*, vol. 2, p. 7 (1949). The serpent says these words to Eve.

CHAPTER 3   You Are the Only Expert on You!

1. Debbie Ford, "You SHOULD Read This," October 11, 2006, *Debbie Ford Newsletter*.
2. Deepak Chopra, *SynchroDestiny* (Wheeling, IL: Nightingale-Conant, 2002), audiobook, Part Four, "The Power of Self-Referral."
3. Neale Donald Walsch, *Conversations with God: An Uncommon Dialogue, Book 1* (New York: G.P. Putnam's Sons, 1996), 44.

CHAPTER 6   Step One: Get Naked

1. Wikipedia, s.v. "Wishful thinking," last modified November 8, 2016, en.wikipedia.org/wiki/Wishful_thinking.
2. Elie Wiesel, "Hope, Despair and Memory" (Nobel Lecture, December 11, 1986), available at nobelprize.org/nobel_prizes/peace/laureates/1986/wiesel-lecture.html.
3. Kevin McSpadden, "You Now Have a Shorter Attention Span Than a Goldfish," *Time*, May 13, 2015, time.com/3858309/attention-spans-goldfish/.

CHAPTER 7   Step Two: Busting Your Own BS

1. Debbie Ford, *The Best Year of Your Life: Dream It, Plan It, Live It* (New York: HarperOne, 2005), 64, 68.

CHAPTER 8   Step Three: Shift Happens

1. Anaïs Nin, *Seduction of the Minotaur* (Chicago: The Swallow Press, 1961), 124.
2. Debbie Ford, *The Right Questions: Ten Essential Questions to Guide You to an Extraordinary Life* (New York: HarperCollins, 2003), 97.

CHAPTER 11   Step Six: Embracing Your Humanity

1. "Don't Believe Everything You Think," Cleveland Clinic Wellness, accessed January 6, 2017, clevelandclinicwellness.com/programs/NewSFN/pages/default.aspx?Lesson=3&Topic=2&UserId=00000000-0000-0000-0000-000000000705.

CHAPTER 12   Step Seven: The Power of I AM

1. Robert Bly, *A Little Book on the Human Shadow*, ed. William Booth (New York: HarperOne, 1988), 18.
2. Debbie Ford, *The Dark Side of the Light Chasers: Reclaiming Your Power, Creativity, Brilliance, and Dreams* (New York: Riverhead Trade, 1998), 140.

CHAPTER 14   The Integrity Protection Program

1. "Jay Leno: The Kennedy Center Mark Twain Prize," televised by PBS on November 23, 2014, pbs.org/mark-twain-prize/shows/2014-show-jay-leno/.

CONCLUSION   The Integrity Promise

1. Bronnie Ware, "Regrets of the Dying" (blog post), November 19, 2009, bronnieware.com/blog/regrets-of-the-dying/.
2. Charles Du Bos, *Approximations* (Paris: 1929), 129, archive.org/stream/approximations03dubouoft#page/128/mode/2up.

About the Author

Kelley Kosow is an author, motivational speaker, and the chief executive officer of the highly acclaimed Ford Institute. She continues the legacy of the late Debbie Ford, *New York Times* bestselling author and creator of The Shadow Process, and leads the development and teachings of The Ford Institute's transformational programs to tens of thousands of people across the globe.

Known as a "kick-ass" coach to high-level executives, change makers, celebrities, and dynamic, motivated individuals committed to personal transformation, Kelley blends her quick wit, laser-sharp insight, and relentless compassion to help people upgrade their lives on a cellular level. While her gifts are many, she is remarkably skilled at awakening people to their limiting patterns, beliefs, and self-sabotaging behaviors and presenting the path of what is possible. Her coaching elevates the relationships her clients and students have not only with others, but also with themselves.

Kelley is a graduate of Brown University and the University of Miami Law School and was formerly a practicing attorney and family law mediator. Though she achieved great success in her career, she felt "stuck" and was seeking more meaningful work when she discovered The Ford Institute. After Kelley began working with Debbie, she knew that a new path had opened up for her, and she became a staff member in 2007.

Prior to that, Kelley founded the company Go Goddess!™ Inc., which created games, books, and seminars to empower, inspire, and entertain women and girls. She has been featured in *O: The Oprah Magazine* as someone who could "Dream it, Do it," as well as in *InStyle*, *People*, *Working Mother*, *Latina*, the *New York Times*, *Conde*

Nast Traveler, and the *Los Angeles Times*. Kelley has also appeared on Lifetime's *The Balancing Act* and the *Better Show*.

Today, Kelley splits her time in Miami, New York City, and Los Angeles with family, friends, and her personal development community.

For more on Kelley and her work, visit kelleykosow.com.

About Sounds True

Sounds True is a multimedia publisher whose mission is to inspire and support personal transformation and spiritual awakening. Founded in 1985 and located in Boulder, Colorado, we work with many of the leading spiritual teachers, thinkers, healers, and visionary artists of our time. We strive with every title to preserve the essential "living wisdom" of the author or artist. It is our goal to create products that not only provide information to a reader or listener, but that also embody the quality of a wisdom transmission.

For those seeking genuine transformation, Sounds True is your trusted partner. At SoundsTrue.com you will find a wealth of free resources to support your journey, including exclusive weekly audio interviews, free downloads, interactive learning tools, and other special savings on all our titles.

To learn more, please visit SoundsTrue.com/freegifts or call us toll-free at 800.333.9185.